Apples, Peaches & Pears

Elizabeth Baird

James Lorimer & Company, Publishers
Toronto 1977

ISBN 0-88862-128-0 paper
       0-88862-129-9 cloth
Cover photo: Karol Ike
Design: Don Fernley
Illustration research: Robert Hill

James Lorimer & Company, Publishers

Egerton Ryerson Memorial Building
35 Britain Street
Toronto

Printed and bound in Canada.

Illustrations courtesy of the T. Eaton Co. and Metropolitan
Toronto Central Library.

Canadian Cataloguing in Publication Data

Baird, Elizabeth, 1939-
    Apples, peaches & pears

ISBN 0-88862-129-9 bd. ISBN 0-88862-128-0 pa.

1. Cookery (Fruit) 2. Cookery, Canadian.
I. Title

TX811.B33   641.6′4   C77-001329-5

CONTENTS

Introduction   5

Cakes   11

Muffins, Quick Breads, Pancakes and Cookies   21

Pies and Pastries   27

Puddings, Ice Creams and Sherbets   41

Pickles, Relishes and Preserves   60

Meat and Fish Main Courses   74

Vegetables   81

Drinks and Candy   85

Varieties   88

Practical Metric Conversion Table   94

Index   95

FOR JANEY

I gratefully acknowledge the assistance of the Ontario Arts Council. I would also like to thank Agriculture Canada, the Nova Scotia Department of Agriculture and Marketing, the Ontario Ministry of Agriculture and Food, the Ontario Food Council especially Mr. E. Chudleigh, the Ontario Fresh Fruit Growers' Marketing Board, the Ontario Apple Marketing Commission and the British Columbia Fruit Growers' Association. They gave kindly of their time and answered numerous questions.

Finally, I thank Angelo Pugliese, who very generously allowed us to take over the Sunkist Fruit Market for a whole sunny September afternoon to photograph the cover.

E.B.

INTRODUCTION

Apples, peaches and pears are Canada's major summer fruits. We grow exceedingly fine varieties of all three, not just in one area, but all across the country. Where temperatures are too cold (especially for peaches), efficient marketing boards maintain supplies as long as possible during the year.

The high quality and abundance of these fruits have given rise to a wide variety of recipes — recipes that show imagination and sensitivity as well as a thrifty ability to deal with a bumper crop in a short season. Apples must hold the record for the number of recipes devoted to them. On the West Coast they are frequently featured with ginger and lemon; on the Prairies with honey, cinnamon and sour cream; in Ontario, in pies, dumplings, cakes, steamed puddings flavoured with nutmeg and cloves and in apple butter; in Quebec with cider, maple syrup and pork; and on the East Coast with spices, molasses and oatmeal. Some recipes are found all over the country, while others appear only in certain areas. The number of recipes for peaches and pears is smaller, but they also offer an amazing variety and reflect an interest in exploiting their special flavours, colours and textures.

Apples, peaches and pears have a long and interesting history of cultivation in Canada, which began when North America's first apple orchard was planted in Nova Scotia centuries ago.

The original French settlers who arrived at Port Royal (now the Annapolis Valley) in 1632 wasted no time in planting orchards, mainly for family use. They continued to plant apple trees as they established settlements along the St. Lawrence and in the Georgian Bay area. These early settlers needed apples for eating and cooking and, since many of them had come from Brittany and Nor-

mandy — areas famous for their cider — they also "needed" the apples for cider production. There is no record of any peach orchards at this time, but it is certain that pear cultivation was practised actively, especially among the French. Pear trees planted in Montreal by the original French settlers flourished in the century between 1750 and 1850 until a bitterly cold winter destroyed them.

When British, American and German settlers joined the French in the backwoods of the Maritimes and in Upper and Lower Canada, they continued the tradition begun by the French and planted apple and pear orchards as they built their homes and established their communities. In the area around Detroit and Niagara, early settlers were quick to realize that the warm climate was ideal for peach growing. One famous resident of the area, Mrs. Simcoe, recorded that in the autumn of 1792 her three peach trees yielded enough fruit for a six-week supply of pies and desserts for the family, plus enough small, flavourful peaches to satisfy the neighbouring young men. She wrote that her share was trifling compared to theirs, and she ate thirty peaches in one day.

The eighteenth and especially the nineteenth centuries were exceptional for experimentation in new fruit varieties. Up to about 1800, most cultivation was done with seedlings, and the chance mating of different strains which often occurred gave the nineteenth century a spectacular range of varieties. In 1881 the Ontario Agricultural Commission listed 84 different varieties of apples. Of the varieties popular today, only the Delicious and Golden Delicious, Wealthy and Cortland were developed after 1850. The Cortland is one of the few apples which was not developed by chance seedling mating. The dissemination of grafting techniques early in the nineteenth century took the chance out of apple cultivation and allowed the propagation of true varieties.

Pears have a similar history of experimentation. Early agricultural journals indicate that many of the varieties popular today — the Bartlett, Beurre d'Anjou, Seckel and Flemish Beauty — were established by the mid-nineteenth century. Another variety common then, the "exceedingly pretty" Clapp's Favourite, was "the" recommended pear by the Fruit Grower's Association of Ontario in 1866. Only the Bosc and Kieffer came later. A look at the names of some of the experimental varieties gives you an idea of the country where much of the pear experimentation was done: Beurre Diel, Grey Doyenne, Beurre Giffard, Duchesse d'Angouleme, Clairgeau and Belle Lucrative.

The problem with growing pears and apples was to find varieties hardy enough to withstand the Canadian winters. Apple stocks were imported from Russia (summer Red Astrachan and Transparent), from Sweden (the very popular Duchess of Oldenburg), from the U.S.A. (Rhode Island Greening, the Northern Spy, Wealthy, Winesap and Yellow Newtown) and of course from England and France. One early native Canadian variety, the Fameuse, Pomme de Neige or Snow Apple, had been around since about 1700. Both it and its descendent, the St. Lawrence, were very hardy apples, well suited to the cold St. Lawrence and Ottawa areas. The Snow Apple was in fact the major nineteenth-century dessert apple, while the Baldwin and Russet were the favourite winter apples and the Red Astrachan, the prime summer apple.

Peach growing was well established in Huron, Essex and Kent counties and on the Niagara Peninsula in Ontario by the 1880s, but none of the varieties is familiar today. Of the sixteen common varieties grown then, the major ones were Crawford's Early and Late. The growers supplied both local *and* regional markets. In the peach-growing centre of Grimsby, Ontario, 70,000 baskets of peaches were shipped from the railway station alone in 1880, and canning plants in the town were processing 150 bushels a day.

But with few exceptions, the early orchards of central and eastern Canada were private, family affairs. Families would plant two to three dozen trees, of which a few would be plum, cherry and pear and the rest apples. Varieties of pears and apples were chosen so that fresh fruit would be available for culinary and dessert purposes from early August until the late fall. Ideally, late varieties would be matured in storage and used throughout the winter until the first strawberries appeared the next spring. Any surplus apples were either dried, made into cider, preserved as sauce or sold on local markets.

Several factors led to a change in the varieties of fruit, especially of apples. The most important of these were the swing away from small family orchards because of more specialized farming and the emergence of large orchards to supply new foreign markets, primarily in Britain. Growers could not afford to cultivate varieties that did not produce a reliable crop every year. Neither could they afford to plant trees that needed a lot of care or that ripened over a long period, because this meant high labour costs. In order to capture new markets, the appearance of the fruit also became increasingly important; red apples tended to edge out yellow or especially green apples and large apples were favoured over small. Later on growers concentrated on finding varieties that maintained their appearance and taste during storage and transportation.

A final and important factor was the impact of the McIntosh and the Delicious. The McIntosh had been around for a long time. Named for John McIntosh who discovered it as a seedling on a partly overgrown farm in Dundas county in Ontario around 1800, the McIntosh proved to be an exceptionally hardy apple. It not only survived in cold eastern Ontario but actually thrived there, and the sunny, cool fall days made its skin red and its flesh crisp. Surprisingly, it was not among the apples recommended for planting in Canada in the 1840s, '50s, '60s or early '70s. Although John, his wife and two sons, Allan and Sandy, had been operating a nursery primarily for the sale of the McIntosh apples since the mid-1830s, it took until the 1890s before the variety became popular. Apparently the McIntosh was susceptible to scab, and it was not until spraying programmes were developed in the 1890s that it became widely and successfully grown.

In British Columbia several attempts to grow fruit commercially were made in the mid-nineteenth century. However, mostly because of cold or lack of water, fruit was not grown commercially with any success until the 1890s, when the first orchards were established in the Okanagan Valley.

By this time the other major apple of the twentieth century had been discovered. Originally grown in Iowa in the 1890s, the Delicious was so named because of its flavour. In 1914, a similar apple with the same distinctive five points on the bottom, but a golden sunshine colour was developed in West Virginia and named the Golden Delicious. Both of these apples have become synonymous with British Columbia because of their success there. Peaches, pears, apricots and cherries all proved to grow well in the Okanagan, too.

The emergence of these three strong varieties — the Delicious, Golden Delicious and the McIntosh — had the effect of muscling out other popular varieties. These three apples are not only juicy, distinctively and brightly coloured (all things which make for market appeal), but also are easier to grow than many varieties. Their trees begin to bear early and do so every year, they grow in a variety of climates and produce large, relatively easy to ship apples that keep well in either a controlled atmosphere or cold storage. All these features appeal to the growers and shippers. Other varieties, like the Wealthy, which come into season at the same time as the McIntosh, were over-

whelmed. The Snow apple, the favourite dessert apple of the nineteenth century, lost out because its trees bore biennially, and the apples, growing on old trees, tended to be small. Still other varieties, such as the Russet, long favoured for its ability to last in storage and make cider, lost out because the three new varieties could be stored even longer. In fact the McIntosh and the Delicious, along with cold and controlled atmosphere storage, have effectively eliminated the need for a variety of apples. The McIntosh, Delicious and Canada's third most popular apple, the Northern Spy, accounted for about 50 per cent of the total crop in 1950 and 72 per cent in 1969. Fifty per cent of all apples grown in 1969 were McIntosh, and it continues to be the most familiar and popular apple today.

With the overwhelming popularity of the Delicious and McIntosh, it has become increasingly difficult to find some of the less commonly grown varieties. A few small growers still market some of the old nineteenth-century favourites — the Russet, Snow, Tolman Sweet, Wealthy, Duchess, Red Astrachan, Wagener, Rhode Island Greening, Gravenstein and Yellow Transparent. Each one has a different colour, aroma, skin texture, flesh, juiciness and taste. Farmers' markets are one likely place to find a wide range of these apples, but supplies will only be maintained if there is a demand. The only other approach is to grow a few trees of your favourite varieties in the backyard.

The varieties of peaches grown in Canada also have changed radically. Beginning in Ontario with the Elberta, introduced in the 1870s, the growers have responded to improved varieties. Ever since the "Haven" peaches were brought from Michigan (Sunhaven, Redhaven, Fairhaven), they have dominated the fresh fruit market. They have a full flavour and fragrance, a lovely red blush and a reasonable shelf life. Other important varieties are the "Vee" peaches (Valiant, Velvet, Vedette, Veteran) developed by the Horticultural Experiment Station in Vineland, Ontario. Because of the climate, 80 per cent of Canada's peaches are grown in Ontario, mainly on the Niagara Peninsula and in Essex and Kent counties. The other 20 per cent are grown in the Okanagan Valley in B.C.

In the 1970s, the full range of apples, peaches and pears are grown in only two areas — the Okanagan Valley of British Columbia and around the southern Great Lakes of Ontario. Apples are produced in large quantities in Quebec, south of Montreal in the area around Rougemont, and Chateauguay, Huntingdon and Musisquoi counties, and apples and pears are grown commercially in the Annapolis, Cornwallis, Kings and Hants valleys of Nova Scotia. Although McIntosh apples are grown in all the major areas, each province has its speciality: British Columbia grows Delicious and Golden Delicious, Spartan, Newtown and Winesap; Ontario has Northern Spy, Cortland and Delicious; Nova Scotia has Gravenstein and Northern Spy; and Quebec has Cortland, Lobo and Snow.

Bartlett is to pears what McIntosh is to apples. In British Columbia a lot of Anjou pears are grown, primarily because the Anjou, like the Bartlett, matures well in storage throughout the winter. For the fresh fruit market, Clapp's Favourite is available in Ontario as well as Keiffer and Bosc, which are also used for canning. Other important varieties are Flemish Beauty and Seckel, although these are more likely to be found on local markets. Most of the pear crop in Nova Scotia is processed and production of pears for this use has maintained a steady level over the last few years. The two most popular varieties are Clapp's Favourite and Bartlett.

Most of the marketing of apples, peaches and pears in Canada is controlled by marketing boards. These are the offspring of growers' associations, in which individual growers, concerned about poor returns and disorderly marketing practices, banded together to form co-operatives. In a situation where world markets are important and where technology is increasingly significant, these or-

ganizations provide the individual grower with the necessary overview and news of technical innovations. Another important factor in fruit growing in Canada has been the government. Federal and provincial departments of agriculture and agricultural schools have worked together to improve and create new varieties and to disseminate information to the fruit growers. Their research into new varieties has helped Canadian growers compete successfully on world markets.

Unfortunately, stiff competition in both world and domestic markets has led to serious problems for consumers. In order to capture their share of the market, Canadian growers must provide fruit that can be picked easily (preferably mechanically), looks attractive, has a long shelf life, transports without bruising and can be stored so that there is a constant, almost year-round supply. This is obviously a tough order. Concern for the "taste" comes after these other priorities, and a variety of tastes is even less important. The tendency for two or three varieties to dominate the market means that one must abandon the supermarket and head for the local farmers' market, road-side stand or small fruit store to enjoy the full range of apples, peaches and pears available.

While the range of varieties has been limited in recent years, the range of processed fruit products has increased dramatically. In the past, apples were made into cider or apple butter or dried. Although dried apples are rarely produced to-day, apple cider is enjoying a resurgence in popularity, especially in Quebec, Ontario and British Columbia.

I have tried most of the ciders currently available in the three cider-producing provinces. The all-over best was Quebec's Lubec, *Saint Antoine-Abbé* for its dryness, full, clean flavour and bouquet. Next was the Cellier St.-Bernard's *Bonsecours Dry Crackling Cider*. Of the sweeter ciders, the Cellier St.-Bernard's *Bonsecours Sweet Crackling* and La Ciderie du Québec's *Rosée Laurentienne Medium Sweet Sparkling Cider* were good, although less successful with food than on their own or in punch. These three ciders have an alcoholic content of between 10 and 11 per cent. The trend in Ontario and British Columbia is to a lower alcoholic content as producers try to find their market. The British Columbia *Growers' Sparkling Cider* (dry), the Andres *Stoney Creek Draft Cider* and *Light and Easy* at between 5 and 6.9 per cent all tasted fine with food, but would be a bit thin on their own. The still wine produced by Chateau Cartier, *Country Roads Apple Wine*, is sweetish with a pronounced apple flavour. It is recommended for a summer drink over ice cubes. The dry and medium ciders are excellent in cooking and can be substituted for dry white wine in recipes.

In addition to these "traditional" uses, processed fruit products now include juices, sauces, relishes, pie fillings and slices (some apples are now being processed in frozen slices). And the Reider Company in St. Catharines, Ontario is using domestic fruits to produce apple brandy, pear "eau de vie" and pear brandy liqueur. A significant proportion of Canada's fruit crop is grown exclusively for processing. For example, Nova Scotia processes 60 per cent of its apple crop and Ontario, about 33 per cent.

Most of the recipes in this book come from old cook books and recipe collections from across the country. Many of these books were the creation of local women's groups. A number of recipes are from family sources which for me means from, in and around Stratford, Ontario and from friends who have generously lent them. Cooking should not be a mysterious process. I have tried to present the recipes as clearly as possible, giving indications of time and appearance whenever possible. I hope you enjoy making these dishes as much as I have. I started this book liking apples, peaches and pears and finished it not only loving them but being astounded by their versatility.

CAKES

Raisin Layer Apple Jack

It's no accident that baking is a strong tradition in Canada. The flour milling companies have played an influential role by regularly publishing cookbooks and distributing them very cheaply or as advertising premiums. The 1915 edition of the *Five Roses Cookbook*, from which Raisin Layer Apple Jack was adapted, is attractive and obviously an expensively made book for the period. The text is interspersed with cartoons of chubby little kids in chefs' hats beating up cakes in giant bowls and tugging away at 98 pound bags of flour. There are testimonials from housewives recounting their success in bread-making with Five Roses flour, and finally, pictures of the bustling mills and grain elevators in Portage La Prairie, Medicine Hat, Keewatin, Brantford and Montreal. Even the bag factory in Winnipeg is pictured.

    4 cups peeled, cored, sliced apples
    1 teaspoon lemon juice
    2 cups sifted all-purpose flour
    2 tablespoons white sugar
    1 teaspoon soda
    1/2 teaspoon baking powder
    1/4 teaspoon salt
    1/4 cup butter
    1 egg, well beaten
    1 cup buttermilk
    1/2 cup raisins
    2/3 cup firmly packed brown sugar
    2 tablespoons melted butter

Sprinkle the apple slices with the lemon juice and set aside.

Sift together the flour, white sugar, soda, baking powder and salt into a large mixing bowl. Using a pastry blender, cut the butter into the sifted dry ingredients until the mixture has the consistency of coarse meal (as for tea biscuits).

Combine the egg and buttermilk. Stir into the dry ingredients and mix only long enough to make a smooth batter.

Place about one-third of the apple slices in the bottom of a buttered 8" × 8" cake pan. Sprinkle on evenly half of the raisins and one-third of the brown sugar. Spoon half the batter over the apple mixture. Repeat with another layer of one-third of the apples and brown sugar, then the remaining raisins and batter. Arrange the rest of the apple slices in neat rows on top of the batter. Sprinkle on the last of the brown sugar and drizzle with the melted butter.

Bake at 400 degrees for 40-45 minutes. The top will puff up, turn a beautiful golden brown, and the edges of the cake will come out from the pan.

A delicious cake, hot from the oven, warm or cool, it is also a good pudding, served hot with heavy cream or Caramel Sauce (see page 59). *Makes 16 pieces.*

Applesauce Cake

    1/2 cup butter
    1 cup firmly packed brown sugar
    2 eggs
    2 cups sifted cake flour
    2 teaspoons baking powder
    1/4 teaspoon soda
    1/2 teaspoon salt
    1/4 teaspoon cloves
    1 teaspoon cinnamon
    1/2 teaspoon allspice
    1/4 teaspoon freshly grated nutmeg
    1 cup raisins
    1 cup Thick Unsweetened Applesauce (see
    page 41)

Cream butter until light and fluffy. Beat in the sugar gradually. Add the eggs 1 at a time, beating after each addition. Sift together the flour, baking powder, soda, salt and spices. Remove 2 tablespoons and dredge the raisins. Reserve.

Add the sifted dry ingredients to the butter mixture in 3 parts, alternating with the applesauce in 2 parts. Begin and end with the dry ingredients. Stir in the dredged raisins.

Bake in a well-greased, lined 9" × 9" cake tin for 50 to 60 minutes at 350 degrees, or until a skewer inserted in the middle comes out clean. Cool and ice with Walnut Rum Butter Icing (see below). *Makes 16 pieces.*

Walnut Rum Butter Icing

    2 tablespoons soft butter
    1 1/4 cups icing sugar
    1 tablespoon rum
    1-2 tablespoons light to heavy cream
    1/3-1/2 cup fresh walnut halves

Cream the butter. Beat in one-third of the icing sugar and all of the rum. Beat in the rest of the icing sugar and as much of the cream as is necessary to make a smooth, creamy icing.

Spread over the cake and arrange the walnut halves on the surface.

There is enough icing for the top of a 8" × 8" or 9" × 9" cake. For a large layer cake, double the quantities.

Apple Meringue Cake

Cake

    Applesauce Cake batter (see above)

Meringue

    2 egg whites
    pinch of cream of tartar
    pinch of salt
    1/2 cup firmly packed brown sugar
    1/2 teaspoon vanilla
    1/2 cup chopped almonds, pecans or fresh
        walnuts

Turn the batter into well-greased 9" × 9" cake pan and set aside.

To make the meringue, beat the egg whites at a low speed until frothy. Sprinkle on the cream of tartar and salt, then increase speed and beat until the egg whites stand in soft peaks. Gradually add the brown sugar while continuing to beat. Stop when the meringue stands in firm peaks. Stir in the vanilla and nuts. Spread over the batter.

Bake at 350 degrees for 1 hour, or until a skewer inserted in the middle comes out clean. Cool in the pan on a rack. *Makes 16 pieces.*

Layered Cinnamon Apple Coffee Cake

    4 cups finely chopped tart apples
    1/3 cup firmly packed brown sugar
    1 1/2 teaspoons cinnamon
    1/2 teaspoon freshly grated nutmeg
    4 eggs
    1 1/2 cups white sugar

1 cup oil
1 tablespoon vanilla
3 cups sifted all-purpose flour
1 tablespoon baking powder
$1/2$ teaspoon salt
$1/4$ cup fresh apple cider or juice

Combine the apples, brown sugar and spices and set aside.

Combine the eggs, white sugar, oil and vanilla in a large mixing bowl. Beat until light, slightly thickened and pale yellow.

Sift together the flour, baking powder and salt. Add half to the egg mixture, then the cider and the remaining dry ingredients. Mix well.

Spoon half of the batter into a well-greased, floured 10″ spring-form tube pan. Spread three-quarters of the apple mixture over the batter, cover with the remaining batter and then an even layer of the apple mixture. Bake at 350 degrees for 1 hour and 10 minutes, or until a skewer inserted in the middle comes out clean.

Cool in the pan for 10 minutes. Remove the sides of the pan or turn out onto a rack to finish cooling. *Makes 12 generous servings.*

Apple and Nut Sour Cream Coffee Cake

Cake

$1/3$ cup butter
$1/2$ cup firmly packed brown sugar
1 egg
1 teaspoon vanilla
$1^1/2$ cups sifted all-purpose flour
$1/2$ teaspoon salt
2 teaspoons baking powder
$1/2$ cup milk
1 cup grated, pared, cored apple

Topping

$1/2$ cup commercial sour cream

1 egg
$2/3$ cup chopped fresh walnuts, pecans or almonds
$1/3$ cup firmly packed brown sugar
$3/4$ teaspoon cinnamon

Cream the butter, add the $1/2$ cup brown sugar and beat until light and fluffy. Beat in the egg and vanilla. Sift together the flour, salt and baking powder. Add to the creamed mixture in 3 parts, alternating with the milk in 2 parts. Stir in the apple. Turn into a well-greased, floured 9″ x 9″ cake pan. Smooth the top.

For the topping, combine the sour cream and egg. Beat briefly and spread over the apple batter. Mix together the remaining ingredients and sprinkle evenly over the cake.

Bake at 375 degrees for 30-35 minutes, or until a skewer inserted in the middle comes out clean. *Serves 10-12.*

Spicy Apple Nut Coffee Cake

1/2 cup firmly packed brown sugar
1/2 cup chopped pecans or fresh walnuts
1/2 teaspoon cinnamon

Make the cake part of the Apple and Nut Sour Cream Coffee Cake. Instead of the sour cream topping, combine the ingredients above and spread them over the batter. Bake at 375 degrees for 30-35 minutes.

Apple Wedge Maple Syrup Upside-Down Cake

3 tablespoons butter
1/2 cup maple syrup
1 tablespoon rum
2 1/4 medium apples, peeled
1/3 cup butter
3/4 cup white sugar
2 eggs, separated
1 1/2 cups sifted all-purpose flour
2 teaspoons baking powder
1/4 teaspoon salt
2/3 cup milk
3/4 cup grated apple

Melt the 3 tablespoons butter in a 8" x 8" cake pan. With a small piece of waxed paper or pastry brush, butter the sides of the pan. Add the syrup, remove from heat and sprinkle in the rum.

Divide the apples in eighths, core and arrange in neat rows in the syrup mixture.

Cream the 1/3 cup butter, add 1/2 cup of the sugar and beat until the mixture is light and fluffy. Beat in the egg yolks, 1 at a time.

Sift together the flour, baking powder and salt. Add to the creamed mixture in 3 parts, alternately with the milk in 2 parts. Stir in the grated apple.

Beat the egg whites until stiff but not dry. Beat in the remaining 1/4 cup of sugar and fold gently into the batter. Spread the batter evenly over the apples.

Bake at 350 degrees for 40-45 minutes, or until the cake springs back when lightly touched. Remove from the oven. Let stand 5 minutes and turn out onto a flat cake plate.

Serve hot or warm with a bowl of lightly-whipped unsweetened cream. *Serves 6-8.*

Apple Ginger Upside-Down Cake

This is a particularly buttery, soft, cake and apple mixture. And while the idea of combining fruit with gingerbread is not novel, this is an especially good example. The cake could be adapted to cover poached or preserved pears with freshly-shelled walnut halves, or fresh or preserved peaches with almonds.

1/4 cup butter
3/4 cup firmly packed brown sugar
3 medium apples
1/3 cup chopped fresh walnuts or pecans
1/4 teaspoon grated lemon rind
1/2 cup butter
1/3 cup firmly packed brown sugar
1 egg
1/4 cup molasses
1 cup sifted all-purpose flour
1 teaspoon baking powder
1/2 teaspoon soda
1/4 teaspoon salt
1 1/4 teaspoons ginger
3/4 teaspoon cinnamon
1/4 teaspoon freshly grated nutmeg
1/8 teaspoon cloves
1/3 cup boiling water

Melt the 1/4 cup butter in a 9" x 9" cake pan. Cool. With a small piece of waxed paper, butter the sides of the pan. Add the 3/4 cup brown sugar and stir over low heat until the sugar begins to melt. Remove from heat and reserve.

Peel the apples. Divide into eighths, core, and arrange in neat rows in the butter-sugar mixture. Sprinkle the nuts and lemon rind evenly over the apples. Set aside.

Cream together the ¹/₂ cup butter with the ¹/₃ cup sugar. Beat in the egg and molasses.

Sift together the flour, baking powder, soda, salt and spices. Stir into the creamed mixture. Rapidly mix in the boiling water. The batter should be smooth but not overworked. Spoon evenly over the apples.

Bake at 350 degrees for 30-35 minutes, or until the gingerbread springs back when lightly touched, and the apples are tender. Remove from the oven and let stand 5 minutes. Turn out onto a flat cake plate. Serve immediately with a bowl of lightly-whipped cream. *Serves 8-10.*

Upside-Down Peach Cake

3 tablespoons butter
1 teaspoon fine cut orange marmalade or ¹/₂
        teaspoon grated orange rind
¹/₃ cup firmly packed brown sugar
4 medium peaches
6 maraschino cherries
¹/₄ cup butter
¹/₂ cup firmly packed brown sugar
1 egg
¹/₄ teaspoon almond extract
1 cup sifted cake flour
1¹/₂ teaspoons baking powder
¹/₄ teaspoon salt
¹/₂ teaspoon cinnamon
¹/₃ cup milk

Melt the 3 tablespoons of butter in an 8″ x 8″ cake pan over low heat. Brush the sides of the pan with butter. Mix in the marmalade and brown sugar. Continue cooking until slightly bubbly. Remove from the heat.

Scald and peel the peaches. Cut into eighths and place in 3-4 parallel rows in the butter-sugar mixture. Sliver the cherries and arrange between the rows of peaches. Reserve.

Cream the ¹/₄ cup butter, add the ¹/₂ cup sugar and beat until light and fluffy. Beat in the egg and almond extract.

Sift together the dry ingredients. Stir half the dry ingredients into the creamed mixture, all the milk and the remaining dry ingredients.

Spread evenly over the peaches (the layer of batter will be quite thin). Bake at 350 degrees for 40-45 minutes, or until a skewer inserted in the middle comes out clean.

Remove from the oven, let stand 5 minutes in the pan and then invert onto a large cake plate.

This cake is good served very fresh, or even better when still warm from the oven, accompanied by a bowl of lightly-whipped unsweetened cream. *Serves 8.*

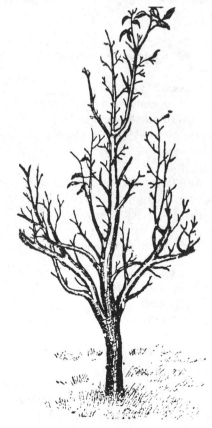

Dutch Apple, Peach or Pear Cake

Dutch Apple Cake is a dessert that cuts across many national boundaries. Variations of it are common in German, Jewish, French and Scandinavian cooking. The fact that it's called Dutch Apple Cake in so many recipe books acknowledges that its origins are in fact German, not Dutch; Dutch in this context is a mistaken translation of Deutsch, meaning German.

Peaches and pears can easily replace the apples in the recipe. Many Dutch Apple Cakes have a baking powder biscuit base or a thin crustier cake bottom. This recipe has a deeper, fluffier butter cake foundation, and the fruit and cinnamon dip into the batter, creating an attractive, uneven texture on top.

1/2 cup butter
1 cup firmly packed brown sugar
1 egg
1 1/2 teaspoons vanilla
1/4 teaspoon grated lemon or orange rind
1 3/4 cups sifted all-purpose flour
1 tablespoon baking powder
1/2 teaspoon salt
3/4 cup milk
3 3/4 cups thinly sliced apples or pears, or 3
    cups thinly sliced peaches
1/3 cup firmly packed brown sugar
1 1/2 teaspoons cinnamon
3 tablespoons melted butter

Cream the 1/2 cup butter, add the cup of brown sugar and beat until light and fluffy. Beat in the egg, vanilla and rind.

Sift together the flour, baking powder and salt. Add to the creamed mixture in 3 parts, alternating with the milk in 2 parts. Begin and end with the dry ingredients.

Turn the batter into a well-greased, floured 9" × 12" cake tin and spread evenly. Lay the fruit slices, like shingles, over the top of the batter.

Combine the remaining brown sugar and cinnamon. Sprinkle over the fruit. Drizzle with the melted butter.

Bake at 350 degrees for 40-45 minutes, or until a skewer inserted in the centre comes out clean. Cool in the pan.

Serve either as a cake or a dessert with sour cream. It is best when very fresh, still warm from the oven. *Serves 10-12.*

Hustling Harvesters' Cake

There can be no doubt from its lively name that this recipe originated in the west.

1/4 cup butter
1/4 cup shortening or lard (the original recipe
    calls for lard)
1 cup firmly packed brown sugar
1 egg
2 cups sifted all-purpose flour
1 teaspoon soda
1/4 teaspoon salt
1/4 teaspoon freshly grated nutmeg
1/4 teaspoon allspice
1 teaspoon cinnamon
3/4 cup finely chopped apples
1 cup sour milk or buttermilk

Cream the butter and shortening until light and fluffy. Beat in the sugar and egg.

Sift together the flour, soda, salt and spices. Remove 2 tablespoons and lightly coat the apples.

Beat the dry ingredients in 3 parts into the creamed mixture, alternating with the milk in 2 parts. Begin and end with the dry. Fold in the apples.

Pour into a well-greased and lightly-floured 9" x 9" cake pan. Spread the batter out thicker at the edges than at the middle.

Bake at 350 degrees for 40 minutes, or until a skewer inserted in the middle comes out clean. Cool on a rack in the pan.

This cake is not too sweet and does not need any

icing if it is to be served informally. Sprinkle with icing sugar if desired or top with Cream Cheese Icing (see below). *Makes 16 pieces.*

Dried Apple Cake

It's a pity that dried apples have become a rarity. They were once the basis of Farmers' Fruit Cake, a cake to be found in cookbooks from coast to coast. In this traditional recipe, home-produced dried apples replaced the expensive (and often unobtainable) store-bought raisins and candied fruit. The following recipe is a version in which molasses is used as part of the sweetening. It's a rich, moist cake, at its best aged a day or so.

> 1 cup dried apples, firmly packed into the cup
> 1 1/2 cups water
> 1/4 cup butter
> 1/2 cup firmly packed brown sugar
> 1 egg
> 1 cup molasses
> 2 cups sifted all-purpose flour
> 1 teaspoon soda
> 1/2 teaspoon salt
> 1 teaspoon cinnamon
> 1/2 teaspoon freshly grated nutmeg
> 1/2 cup buttermilk or sour milk

Place the apples in a bowl, add the water, cover lightly and soak overnight. Place in a saucepan, cover and cook over moderate heat for 20-30 minutes, or until the apples are very tender but not broken up. Remove the lid and continue cooking until all the liquid has evaporated. Cool and chop medium-fine. Set aside.

Cream the butter, add the sugar and beat until the mixture is fluffy. Beat in the egg and molasses.

Sift together the dry ingredients. Add in 3 parts to the creamed mixture, alternately with the milk in 2 parts. Begin and end with the dry ingredients. Be careful not to overbeat. Stir in the chopped apples.

Pour the batter into a well-greased, floured 10" × 10" cake pan. Bake at 350 degrees for 40-45 minutes, or until a skewer inserted in the centre comes out clean. Cool in the pan. If desired, ice with Cream Cheese Icing (see below). *Makes 16 pieces.*

Cream Cheese Icing

> 1 tablespoon soft butter
> 4 ounces cream cheese, at room temperature
> 1 teaspoon grated orange or lemon rind
> 2 1/2 cups icing sugar
> 3 tablespoons light to heavy cream

Cream together the butter and cheese. Work in the rind. Gradually add the icing sugar and cream, beating well to make a spreading consistency. Add more cream or sugar if desired.

Makes enough for the top and sides of a large layer cake. For the top of a single-layer cake, use half a recipe.

Peach Cream Delight

6 cups neatly sliced peaches
1 tablespoon lemon juice
1/4 cup medium-dry sherry
1/4 cup white sugar
1/3 cup water
1 cup white sugar
2 egg yolks
1 cup heavy cream
1/2 teaspoon almond extract
1 9"-10" Sponge Cake, baked in a tube pan
    (see below)

Combine the first 4 ingredients. Cover and let stand 1 hour at room temperature.

Bring the water and 1 cup sugar to the boil in a saucepan. Cook to soft ball stage (225 degrees on a candy thermometer).

Beat the egg yolks until pale yellow. Gradually pour the hot syrup onto the yolks, beating constantly until the mixture has thickened. Place the bowl in a pan filled with ice cubes. Continue to beat at high speed until the mixture is very cold. Add more ice if necessary.

Whip the cream until it mounds but is not stiff. For best results, keep the bowl containing the whipped cream in a pan of ice. Gradually beat the egg yolk mixture into the whipped cream. By the time it is all added, the mixture should stand in firm peaks. Add almond extract and keep cold.

Brush any crumbs off the cake. Place in the centre of a large serving plate. Drain the peaches and sprinkle the liquid onto the cake. Fill the centre of the cake with peaches. Spread the cream over the top and sides of the cake. Arrange the remaining peaches attractively around the cake. Serve as soon as possible. *Serves 10-12.*

Sponge Cake

1 cup sifted cake flour
1/8 teaspoon salt
3 eggs, separated
1 cup white sugar
1/4 cup orange juice
1/4 teaspoon grated orange rind

Sift the flour and salt together 4 times.

Beat the egg whites, adding half of the sugar slowly until the mixture is stiff.

Beat the egg yolks until they are light yellow and form a ribbon when a spoon is drawn out of them. Beat in the remaining sugar. Fold the yolks into the whites and add the juice and rind. Fold in the flour until just blended.

Turn into an ungreased 9" tube pan or two 8" ungreased layer pans. Run a knife across the cake through the batter 5-6 times.

Bake at 350 degrees for 35 minutes for the tube, 20-25 minutes for the layers. The cake should spring back when lightly touched.

Invert the tube cake over a bottle, or turn the layers over a rack. Cool, loosen with a knife and remove from the pans.

Classic Peach Shortcake

5 cups neat peach slices
1/4 cup liquid honey or white sugar
1/4 teaspoon grated orange rind
1 teaspoon orange or peach liqueur
    (optional)
1/2 pint heavy cream
1 teaspoon white sugar
2 drops almond extract or rose water
1 Classic Butter Cake (see page 19)

Lightly stir together the peach slices, honey, orange rind and liqueur. Cover and let stand about 1 hour for juices to form.

Whip the cream then stir in the sugar and almond extract.

Split the butter cake in half horizontally, spoon half the peaches and all of the juice over the bottom layer. Put on the top of the cake and spread the top and sides of the cake with cream. Arrange the remaining slices attractively over the top. Serve immediately. *Enough for 10 people.*

Classic Butter Cake

½ cup soft butter
1 cup white sugar
2 eggs
1 teaspoon vanilla
1½ cups sifted cake and pastry flour
2 teaspoons baking powder
½ teaspoon salt
¾ cup milk

Cream the butter, add the sugar gradually and beat until the mixture is light and fluffy. Beat in the eggs 1 at a time. Add the vanilla. For a light texture, it is important to beat the cake at this stage of its making.

Sift together the dry ingredients. Add the dry ingredients in 3 parts to the creamed mixture, alternating with the milk in 2 parts. Turn into a well-greased 8″ x 8″ cake tin, with the bottom lined in waxed paper. Press the batter up towards the sides, leaving the centre shallower than the sides.

Bake at 350 degrees for 40 minutes, or until a skewer comes out clean. Cool 10 minutes in the pan. Turn out onto a rack to finish cooling. Peel off the waxed paper. This cake is best when very fresh. If it is necessary to make it in advance, wrap it well as soon as it has cooled and store it in an airtight container. It freezes well.

Apple Butter Sponge Roll

Cake

2/3 cup raisins
2 tablespoons rum, brandy, cider or water
3 eggs, separated
3/4 cup white sugar
1/2 cup Thick Unsweetened Applesauce (see page 41)
1 cup sifted cake flour
1/2 teaspoon baking powder
1/2 teaspoon soda
1/4 teaspoon salt
1/2 teaspoon cinnamon
1/4 teaspoon allspice, cloves or freshly grated nutmeg
icing sugar

Filling and Icing

1 1/4 cups heavy cream
1 teaspoon white sugar
1 teaspoon rum or vanilla
1/2 cup apple butter

Place the raisins and 2 tablespoons of rum in a small heavy-bottomed saucepan. Cover and place over very low heat to plump for 10 minutes. Cool.

Beat the egg whites until they stand in soft peaks. Continue beating, add 3/4 cup white sugar gradually until the whites stand in firm, glossy peaks.

Beat the egg yolks until straw coloured. Drain and dry the raisins on paper towelling. Fold into the egg whites along with the yolks and applesauce.

Sift together the flour, baking powder, soda, salt and spices. Fold into the egg white mixture.

Turn into a well-greased and waxed paper-lined jelly roll pan, 15" × 10", and bake at 400 degrees for 10 minutes. The cake will spring back when lightly touched.

Sprinkle a clean tea towel liberally with icing sugar. Turn the cake out onto the tea towel, peel off the waxed paper lining and roll up horizontally to cool.

To assemble, whip the cream, sweetened with the remaining sugar and add rum. Unroll the cake and spread on the apple butter. Spread about one-third of the cream over the apple butter. Roll up again and place on an oval serving platter. Spread the remaining whipped cream over the outside of the roll and mark with the tines of a fork.

Keep chilled and serve as soon as possible. It *is* possible to make the cake part of the sponge roll a half a day or so in advance and keep it rolled up in an air-tight container. But this type of cake tends to go stale rapidly if not properly stored. *Makes about 12 servings.*

MUFFINS, QUICK BREADS, PANCAKES AND COOKIES

Apple Nut Muffins

Muffins

> 2 cups sifted all-purpose flour
> 3 $1/2$ teaspoons baking powder
> $1/2$ teaspoon salt
> $1/4$ teaspoon freshly grated nutmeg
> $1/2$ cup white sugar
> 1 egg, well beaten
> 1 cup milk
> $1/3$ cup melted and cooled butter
> $1/2$ teaspoon vanilla
> $3/4$ cup peeled, grated apple
> 1 cup chopped pecans or fresh walnuts,
> chopped dates, raisins or figs

Topping

> 1 teaspoon cinnamon
> $1/4$ teaspoon cloves
> $1/4$ teaspoon mace
> 1 tablespoon white sugar

Sift the first 5 ingredients together into a large mixing bowl.

Beat together the egg, milk, vanilla and butter in another bowl. Add to the dry ingredients, stirring briefly just to blend. Quickly mix in the apples and nuts.

Spoon into 12 well-greased muffin tins.

Mix together the ingredients for the topping and sprinkle evenly over the tops of the muffins.

Bake at 375 degrees for 25-30 minutes, or until they spring back when lightly touched and have come away from the sides of the tins.

Serve hot with plenty of butter and jam.

Applesauce Streusel Muffins

Batter

> 1 $1/2$ cups sifted all-purpose flour
> $1/4$ cup white sugar
> 1 tablespoon baking powder
> $1/2$ teaspoon salt
> $1/2$ teaspoon cinnamon
> $1/8$ teaspoon allspice or cloves
> 1 egg
> $3/4$ cup milk
> $1/4$ cup melted butter, cooled

Topping

> $1/4$ cup Thick Unsweetened Applesauce (see
> page 41)
> $1/2$ cup firmly packed brown sugar
> $1/3$ cup sifted all-purpose flour
> 2 tablespoons butter

Sift together the dry ingredients for the batter into a mixing bowl. In another bowl, beat together the egg, milk and melted butter. Stir into the dry ingredients, mixing just enough to blend. Turn into well-greased large muffin tins, filling each two-thirds full. Make a small well in the top of each muffin and add 1 teaspoon applesauce.

Combine the brown sugar and flour for the topping. Work in the butter until the mixture is crumbly. Sprinkle a large spoonful on the top of each muffin, keeping it to the centre if possible.

Bake at 400 degrees for 20 minutes or until golden brown. Remove from the muffin tins immediately, scraping up all bits of the streusel topping, and cool on a rack. *Makes 12 large muffins.*

Cranberry Apple Bread

1/2 cup butter
1 cup white sugar
1 egg, well beaten
2 cups sifted all-purpose flour
1 teaspoon soda
1/2 teaspoon salt
1/2 teaspoon cinnamon
1/2 cup milk
1 1/4 cups peeled, cored, grated apple
1/2 cup raw chopped cranberries
1/2 teaspoon grated orange rind

Cream the butter, add the sugar and beat until light and fluffy. Beat in the egg.

Sift together the flour, soda, salt and cinnamon. Add alternately with the milk to the creamed mixture, beginning and ending with the dry ingredients. Stir in the apples, cranberries and rind.

Turn into a well-greased, floured 9" × 5" loaf tin. Bake at 350 degrees for 50 minutes, or until a skewer inserted in the middle comes out clean.

Cool in the pan 10 minutes. Remove from the pan and cool on a rack. Wrap and store for 1 day before using. Cut into 1/2" slices and butter.

Apple Nut or Apple Raisin Bread

Make the bread according to the Cranberry Apple Bread, substituting 3/4 cup raisins or fresh, chopped walnuts or pecans for the cranberries, and 1 teaspoon grated lemon rind for the orange rind.

Molasses Hot Applesauce Bread

This is a very fine Maritime recipe for an unusual bread. Even though there is quite a heady smell of molasses as the bread cooks, molasses does not dominate the flavour. This bread is a very rich dark brown and rises up in a characteristic hump along the middle. It's awfully good in thin slices with cream cheese.

2 cups finely sliced apples
1 tablespoon water
3 tablespoons shortening or butter
1/2 cup molasses
1 egg
1 1/2 cups sifted all-purpose flour
1 teaspoon soda
1/2 teaspoon salt
1 cup rolled oats
1/2 cup buttermilk
1 cup raisins

Place the apples and water in a saucepan over low heat. Cover tightly and cook, stirring and mashing from time to time, until the apples are tender and smooth. There should be 1 cup of applesauce. Keep warm.

Cream the shortening, beat in the molasses and then the egg.

Sift together the flour, soda and salt. Mix together with the rolled oats.

Working as quickly as possible, stir the applesauce into the creamed mixture, followed by the dry ingredients in 3 parts, alternately with the buttermilk in 2 parts. Mix in the raisins. Immediately turn the mixture into a buttered 9" × 5" loaf tin and bake at 375 degrees for 50-55 minutes, or until a skewer inserted in the middle comes out clean.

Cool in the pan for 10 minutes. Turn out onto a rack to finish cooling. Wrap and store for 1 day before using. Cut into about 20 slices.

Cider Pound Cake

This pound cake is worth every egg and ounce of butter it calls for. It's the sort of cake that gets made over and over again, partly because of its taste which gets better after a few days, and partly because of its firm but light texture. Serve it sliced, plain or toasted, with lots of butter and cups of lemon tea.

    1 cup butter
    $1^1/_2$ cups firmly packed brown sugar
    4 eggs
    3 cups sifted all-purpose flour
    1 teaspoon soda
    $^1/_4$ teaspoon salt
    $^3/_4$ teaspoon freshly grated nutmeg or $^1/_2$
        teaspoon ground cardamom
    1 cup fresh cider

Cream the butter until fluffy and beat in the sugar a little at a time. Add the eggs, beating well after each addition. The mixture should be very creamy.

Sift together the flour, soda, salt and nutmeg.

Add the dry ingredients alternately with the cider. Beat until smooth after each addition. Working quickly, pour the batter into a greased 9″ × 5″ loaf pan.

Bake at 350 degrees for 1 hour, or until a skewer inserted in the middle comes out clean. Cool in the pan for 10 minutes and finish cooling on a rack. Wrap and store in an air-tight container. *Makes about 20 slices.*

Apple Butter Pound Cake

    $^1/_2$ cup butter
    1 cup sugar
    3 eggs
    $2^1/_2$ cups sifted all-purpose flour
    $1^1/_2$ teaspoons soda
    $^1/_2$ teaspoon salt
    1 teaspoon cinnamon
    $^1/_2$ teaspoon each of nutmeg and cloves
    1 cup buttermilk or sour milk
    1 cup apple butter
    $^1/_3$ cup finely chopped fresh walnuts or
        pecans

Cream the butter, add the sugar and beat until the mixture is light and fluffy. Add the eggs 1 at a time, beating well after each addition.

Sift together the flour, soda, salt and spices. Add to the creamed mixture in 3 parts, alternating with the buttermilk in 2 parts. Stir in the apple butter.

Turn into a well-greased, lined 9″ × 5″ loaf tin. Sprinkle the nuts over the top and press in lightly with the back of a spoon.

Bake at 350 degrees for 1 hour and 10 minutes, or until a skewer inserted in the middle comes out clean.

Cool in the pan for 10 minutes. Remove from the pan and cool on a rack. Wrap and store for 1 day before slicing. Cut into about 20 slices and butter.

Peach Doughnuts

2 teaspoons white sugar
1/4 cup lukewarm water
2 teaspoons active dry yeast (1 envelope)
2 cups milk
1/3 cup shortening
1/2 cup white sugar
1/2 teaspoon freshly grated nutmeg
1/2 teaspoon grated orange rind
1/2 teaspoon vanilla
1 1/2 teaspoon salt
1 egg, well beaten
6-6 1/2 cups all-purpose flour
3 peaches
1 1/2 cups icing sugar
2-3 tablespoons orange juice

Dissolve the 2 teaspoons of sugar in the water. Sprinkle the yeast over the top. Let stand for 10 minutes, allowing the yeast to bubble up. Stir with a fork.

Meanwhile, combine the milk, shortening and 1/2 cup sugar in a saucepan. Stir. Heat just long enough to melt the shortening. Pour into a large mixing bowl. Cool to lukewarm, add the nutmeg, rind, vanilla, salt and egg. Beat in the yeast mixture and 2 cups of the flour. Cover the bowl with a damp tea towel and let rise in a warm place until spongy, about 1 hour.

Stir in another cup or so of the flour. Turn out onto a generously floured board and knead in as much of the remaining flour as is necessary to make a workable dough. Knead 8-10 minutes or until the dough is smooth and elastic.

Place in a large well-greased bowl, turning the dough over to grease all sides. Cover the dough with a round of waxed paper and the bowl with a damp towel. Put in a warm place until the dough has doubled in bulk, about 1-1 1/2 hours.

Peel, stone and slice the peaches into sixteenths. Place on paper towelling.

Punch down the dough and divide into 2 parts. Roll each part into a sausage shape, about 28" long and 1 1/2" in diameter. Cut off a piece 1"-1 1/4" long, press flat with the fingers and place a slice of peach in the middle. Press the edges of the dough together. Use a light dust of flour on the fingers if necessary. Shape into a smooth ball. Place 2" apart, on a well-floured baking sheet. Cover lightly. Let rise until doubled in bulk, about 1 hour.

Fry 4 at a time in deep fat at 360 degrees. They need about 2 minutes on each side to cook in the middle. Drain on paper towels on a rack.

Combine the icing sugar and enough of the orange juice to form a runny icing. Pour a little over each doughnut as a glaze. *Makes about 40 doughnuts.*

Peach Fritters

A lot of people hesitate to make fritters because they're afraid of deep frying. But fritters are not difficult to make and the results are delicious, especially with fresh peaches and apples. The trick is to regulate the temperature of the fat so that the fritter batter cooks through before the outside burns and to use paper towels to help drain the fat.

6 peaches
2 tablespoons white sugar
1 tablespoon peach brandy or orange liqueur
     (optional)

Batter

1 cup sifted all-purpose flour
1/2 teaspoon salt
1/2 teaspoon baking powder
1 teaspoon white sugar
1/2 teaspoon grated orange rind
2 eggs, separated
1/2 cup milk
1 tablespoon melted, cooled butter

Garnish

1/4 cup white sugar
1 teaspoon cinnamon
or

Maple Butter Sauce (see below)

Peel and stone the peaches and divide them into quarters. Sprinkle on the 2 tablespoons sugar and brandy and let stand covered an hour.

Sift the dry ingredients for the batter into a mixing bowl. Add the rind. Whisk the egg yolks, milk and butter and stir them into the dry ingredients.

Beat the egg whites until stiff but not dry and fold them into the batter.

Drain the peach slices thoroughly, using some of the liquid for the sauce or another purpose.

Add the peaches to the batter and fry by the large spoonful in fat at 360 degrees, 1½ minutes on each side. Include a portion of the peach in each fritter. Drain well on paper towels. Combine the white sugar and cinnamon and sprinkle over the fritters, or serve with Maple Butter Sauce (see below). *Makes 12 servings of 2 fritters each.*

Maple Butter Sauce

1 cup maple syrup
2 tablespoons butter
a few gratings of nutmeg

Heat all ingredients together in a saucepan until the butter is melted. Serve hot in a pitcher.

Apple or Peach Pancakes

1 cup sifted all-purpose flour
2 teaspoons baking powder
¼ teaspoon salt
1 teaspoon white sugar
a few gratings of nutmeg (optional)
1 egg
¾-1 cup milk
1½ tablespoons melted butter
½ cup peeled, cored and grated apple or ½
    cup very finely chopped peaches

Sift the dry ingredients together into a medium-sized mixing bowl.

Beat together the egg and ¾ cup milk. Stir into the dry ingredients, making a smooth batter. Add the melted butter and fruit.

For a thinner pancake, add up to ¼ cup more milk.

Pour onto a preheated, buttered griddle or frying pan, using about ¼ cup batter for each pancake. Turn the pancakes when the bubbles break and do not fill in. Cook on the other side for about 30-45 seconds.

Serve hot with maple syrup, softened butter and lean bacon or sausages. *Makes enough for 4.*

Apple Rolled Oats Squares

1½ cups sifted all-purpose flour
¼ teaspoon soda
¼ teaspoon salt
1 cup firmly packed brown sugar
1½ cups rolled oats
¾ cup butter
2¾ cups thinly sliced apples
3 tablespoons melted butter
¾ teaspoon cinnamon
2 teaspoons lemon juice
¼ teaspoon grated lemon rind

Sift the first 3 ingredients together into a large mixing bowl. Mix in the brown sugar and rolled oats. Using a pastry blender or 2 knives, cut the butter into the dry ingredients until the mixture is crumbly. Press half of this mixture into the bottom of a well-greased 9" x 9" cake tin. Reserve the rest.

Combine the remaining ingredients in a bowl. Lightly toss to coat the apple slices evenly. Spread over the rolled oats base and sprinkle the remaining crumbs over the top in an even layer. Press down gently.

Bake at 375 degrees for 40-45 minutes or until the crumb topping is golden brown and the apples tender when pierced with the tip of a pointed knife. *Makes 16 squares.*

Apple and Nut Squares

This recipe, which originally appeared in a Maritime cookbook, is the best apple "cookie" recipe I've come across.

Filling

>1 tablespoon butter
>2 cups thin apple slices
>1/2 cup white sugar
>1/2 teaspoon grated lemon rind
>2 tablespoons lemon juice
>1 egg, beaten

Base

>1 cup sifted all-purpose flour
>2 tablespoons brown sugar
>1/3 cup soft butter

Topping

>3/4 cup firmly packed brown sugar
>1 tablespoon soft butter
>1 egg, beaten
>1/2 cup chopped almonds

Melt the butter for the filling in a heavy-bottomed saucepan over low heat. Add the apples, white sugar, lemon rind and juice. Stir gently. Increase the heat slightly so that the mixture bubbles but does not burn and cook until the liquid is reduced and the apples translucent. Remove from the heat. Cool and gently mix with the beaten egg. Set aside.

Combine the flour and sugar for the base. Mix in the butter. Press this crumbly mixture evenly into the bottom of a well-greased 8" x 8" cake tin. Spread on the apple mixture.

Blend together the brown sugar for the topping and the remaining butter. Mix in the egg and then the almonds. Spread over the apple mixture. Don't worry if the 2 top layers seem to blend a bit.

Bake at 350 degrees for 30 minutes or until golden brown on top and firm to the touch. Cool in the pan. *Makes 16 squares.*

Applesauce Spice Hermits

>2/3 cup butter
>1 cup firmly packed brown sugar
>1 egg
>1/4 cup molasses or corn syrup
>1 3/4 cups sifted all-purpose flour
>1 1/2 teaspoons baking powder
>1/2 teaspoon soda
>1/2 teaspoon salt
>1/4 teaspoon allspice
>3/4 teaspoon cinnamon
>1/4 teaspoon cloves
>1/8 teaspoon ginger
>1/2 teaspoon mace
>1 cup Thick Unsweetened Applesauce (see page 41)
>1/2 cup chopped nuts
>3/4 cup mixed cut peel
>1 1/2 cups seeded raisins

Cream the butter, add the brown sugar and beat until light and fluffy. Beat in the egg and then the molasses.

Sift together the flour, baking powder, soda, salt and spices. Mix in 3 parts into the creamed batter alternately with the applesauce in 2 parts. Begin and end with the dry ingredients. Stir in the remaining ingredients.

Drop by teaspoonfuls 2" apart onto greased baking sheets. Bake at 375 degrees for 12-13 minutes or until browned on the bottom and springy on top. Cool on a rack.

These cookies are good keepers and in fact taste better after a day or so of maturing. *Yields 5-6 dozen.*

PIES AND PASTRIES

A Canadian recipe book without a good section on pies would be inconceivable. From our earliest cookbooks meat, fish, vegetable and fruit pies have been omnipresent. The earliest English-language Canadian cookbook, *The Cook Not Mad or Rational Cookery*, has no fewer than 9 recipes for pastry alone. Interestingly enough, it was Canadians who popularized the pie with a top and bottom crust. These pies were convenient noon meals and easier to carry back to the clearings than the British single-crust pies. It was also a common Canadian practice to make pies with 3 or 4 layers of pastry, with fillings between each. Real stick-to-the-ribs stuff.

None of the following pies is meant just to be hearty. They are examples of Canadian pie-making at its best.

When calculating how much pastry you'll need for pies, figure roughly that 2 cups of flour will make 24 tart shells, 1 two-crust 9″-10″ pie or 2 one-crust pie shells of 9″-10″.

Hot Water Pastry

This is a good simple pastry and is at its best when very fresh.

> $2/3$ cup shortening at room temperature
> $1/3$ cup boiling water
> $3/4$ teaspoon salt
> 2 cups minus 2 tablespoons sifted
>   all-purpose flour

Place the shortening in a mixing bowl. Pour on the boiling water and beat with a fork until cool, creamy and fluffy, like face cream.

Blend together the salt and flour and work into the shortening until the pastry forms a ball. Divide into 2 balls and wrap in waxed paper. Chill. Use within a day or two.

Let the pastry come to room temperature before rolling out on a well-floured counter or pastry cloth.

Standard Pastry

This is the standard pastry recipe, although quite rich in fat. I advise the use of all-purpose flour as it's easier to handle. Experts in this pastry recipe are said to have a "deft" hand.

> 2 cups sifted all-purpose flour or $2^1/4$ cups
>   sifted pastry flour
> 1 teaspoon salt
> $3/4$ cup cold shortening
> $1/4$-$1/3$ cup cold water

Combine the flour and salt in a mixing bowl. Using a pastry blender or 2 knives cut in the shortening. When the flour and shortening mixture has the consistency of coarse oatmeal with a few large pieces, begin to add the water. Sprinkle on, a tablespoon at a time, always putting it on the dry flour and blending in with a fork. Add only enough water to make the dough hold together. Press into a ball. Divide in 2, wrap each ball in waxed paper and chill. Let the pastry return to room temperature before rolling out on a lightly-floured counter or pastry cloth.

For cheddar cheese pastry, add $1/4$ cup grated old cheddar cheese to the flour before cutting in the shortening.

Classic Apple Pie

Apple pie as it's sold in supermarkets, most bakeries and restaurants is enough to give Canadian cooking a bad name. This is disappointing because a fine apple pie is very easy to make and tastes terrific. What relation to real pie are these crusted things heaped up in the middle with glutinous bright yellow pie "filling?" Only the colour lets you know it's apple, not cherry.

Certain apples are well suited to this classic pie. I recommend any of the August apples, especially the Red Astrachan or Transparent, and then Duchess, Melba, Cortland and Northern Spy.

> sufficient pastry for a two-crust 9" pie
> 6 cups sliced apples
> 1/2 cup white sugar (3/4 cup if the apples are very tart)
> 1/2 teaspoon cinnamon or 1/8 teaspoon freshly grated nutmeg or 1/2 teaspoon rose water
> 1 1/2 tablespoons butter
> 1 egg white slightly beaten or 1 tablespoon milk
> 1 teaspoon white sugar
> Cheddar cheese

Line a pie plate with pastry. Do not trim. Roll out pastry for top crust.

Combine apples, 1/2 cup sugar and flavouring in a bowl. Toss lightly to distribute sugar. Wet the pastry on the rim of the pie plate with water. Add the apples, heaping them up in the middle. Dot with butter. Put on the top crust and press the crust around the edge. Trim and flute. Slash decorative steam holes in the top crust. Brush with lightly-beaten egg white or milk and sprinkle with 1 teaspoon sugar.

Bake at 450 degrees for 10 minutes. Reduce heat to 350 degrees for 40-50 minutes or until the pie is golden brown and the apples tender. Serve with wedges of well-aged Cheddar cheese. Serves 6.

Classic Peach Pie

> sufficient pastry for a two-crust 9" pie
> 5 cups peeled, stoned, sliced peaches
> 2 teaspoons lemon juice
> 1/4 teaspoon almond extract (optional)
> 2/3 cup white sugar
> pinch of salt
> 2 tablespoons cornstarch
> 1/4 teaspoon freshly grated nutmeg or 1/2 teaspoon cinnamon (optional)
> 2 tablespoons butter
> 1 teaspoon light cream or milk
> 1 teaspoon white sugar

Put the peaches in a large bowl and sprinkle with the lemon juice and almond extract. Combine the 2/3 cup sugar, salt, cornstarch and spices in another bowl. Mix into the peaches, coating them evenly. Turn the peaches into the untrimmed pie shell. Dot the fruit with butter.

Wet the pastry on the rim of the pie plate. Cover the fruit with the top crust. Let the top fit loosely over the peaches and press along the dampened edge to join the 2 layers of pastry together. Trim both crusts off approximately 1/2" past the rim of the pie plate, then turn the crusts back over the rim, flute attractively, pressing the pastry together as you do so.

Brush the top of the pie with the cream, sprinkle with 1 teaspoon sugar and slash in 6 places near the centre of the top crust.

Bake at 450 degrees for 15 minutes. Reduce the heat to 350 and bake 30-35 minutes more, or until both crusts are bronzed, the peaches tender and the juices running. (Not over the bottom of your oven, I hope.)

Serve warm with vanilla ice cream, whipped cream or just as it is. *Serves 6.*

Golden Honey Pear Pie

The original nineteenth-century recipe for this pie called for pears "ripe and mellow enough to eat." They should, in fact, be so mellow that "from the taste, it might be called honey pie." Juicy, ripe Bartlett pears are excellent.

>sufficient pastry for a deep two-crust 9" pie
>4 ripe, juicy pears
>$1/3$ cup liquid honey
>2 teaspoons flour
>1 tablespoon butter
>$1/4$ cup slivered blanched almonds (optional)

Peel and core pears. Cut in eighths and lay in the pie shell. Drizzle on the honey, shake on the flour and dot the top with butter. Sprinkle the almonds over the pears.

Dampen the pastry on the rim of the pie plate. Place the top crust over the pears, trim and press the edges together. Flute and slash 6-8 steam holes in the top. Bake at 350 degrees for 45 minutes. *Serves 6.*

Deep Dish Apple Pie

>6 large apples
>$1/2$ cup water
>$1/4$ cup firmly packed brown sugar
>$1/2$ teaspoon cinnamon
>$1/2$ cup white sugar
>$1/2$ teaspoon grated lemon peel
>2 tablespoons lemon juice
>1 tablespoon butter
>sufficient pastry to cover one deep 9"
>   ovenproof dish
>1 teaspoon beaten egg
>1 teaspoon water
>1 teaspoon white sugar

Wash, peel, core and slice the apples. Simmer the peelings and cores with the $1/2$ cup water in a covered saucepan for 10 minutes. Press out the juice, using a sieve and spoon, and combine with the brown sugar and cinnamon. Simmer again long enough to dissolve the sugar.

Arrange the apples in 2 layers in the ovenproof dish, putting $1/4$ cup of the white sugar and half the grated lemon peel and juice over each layer. Dot with butter and pour the warm apple juice over the top. Cover with pastry. Slit the pastry decoratively and press it all around the sides of the dish using a fork.

Combine the beaten egg and 1 teaspoon water. Brush over the top. Sprinkle with the 1 teaspoon sugar.

Bake at 425 degrees for 15 minutes. Reduce heat to 375 and bake 30 minutes, or until the crust is golden brown and the apples are tender. *Enough for 10-12 servings.*

Deep Dish Fresh Peach Pie

This is a pie big enough for a dozen picnickers. The pastry recipe makes a particularly flaky topping.

Pastry

2 cups sifted all-purpose flour
3/4 teaspoon salt
3/4 cup shortening
1/3 cup ice water
1/4 cup sifted all-purpose flour

Filling

6 cups peeled, stoned, sliced peaches
1 tablespoon lemon juice
2/3 cup firmly packed brown sugar
3 tablespoons flour
pinch of salt
1/4 cup orange juice or water
1/4 cup melted butter

Glaze

1 teaspoon light cream or milk
1 teaspoon white sugar

Combine the 2 cups flour for the pastry with the 3/4 teaspoon salt in a large mixing bowl. Cut the shortening into the flour using a pastry blender or 2 knives. The mixture should look like very coarse oatmeal. Mix the water with the remaining flour for the pastry and make a smooth paste. Stir into the flour and shortening, using a fork to press the pastry together. If necessary, sprinkle a little more cold water onto the dry parts in the bowl. Form into a ball, wrap and cool 30 minutes.

Place the peaches in a large mixing bowl and sprinkle with the lemon juice. Combine the sugar, flour and salt for the filling and toss gently with the peaches to coat all the slices evenly. Spoon into a 9" × 12" ovenproof baking dish. Pour the juice and melted butter evenly over the peaches.

Roll the pastry out into a rectangle large enough to cover the baking dish to a thickness of 3/8". Place over the peaches in the dish, allowing the pastry to hang loosely rather than stretching it over the edges. Trim around the edge and press the pastry to the dish with a fork.

Brush the top of the pastry with the cream and sprinkle with the remaining sugar. Slash 6 holes in the pastry to allow the steam to escape.

Bake at 425 degrees for 15 minutes, reduce the heat to 350 degrees and continue cooking for 40 minutes, or until the crust has turned golden and the juices have begun to run up through the slash holes.

Best served while still warm, on its own or with vanilla ice cream or cream. *Serves 10-12.*

Rich Mincemeat Pie

sufficient pastry for a two-crust 9" pie (see page 27)
3 cups Rich Mincemeat (see page 72)
1 tablespoon brandy or rum
2 tablespoons butter

Line the pie plate with pastry. Do not trim the edges. Spoon the mincemeat into the pie shell, heaping it up slightly in the middle. Sprinkle on the brandy and dot with butter.

Wet the pastry on the rim of the pie plate with water. Place the top crust over the mincemeat. Trim the pastry, press together and flute. Slash 6-8 steam holes in the top crust.

Bake at 425 degrees for 10 minutes. Reduce heat to 350 degrees and continue baking 30 minutes longer, or until the crust is golden brown and the mincemeat bubbles up through the steam holes.

Best served while still warm with a custard sauce (see page 42), whipped cream or vanilla ice cream. Mincemeat pie freezes well, but should be thawed and reheated and cut into small rich wedges before serving. *Serves 6-8.*

Fruit Mincemeat Pie

Proceed as for the Rich Mincemeat Pie, using a 10" pie plate and the same quantity of brandy and butter. To the mincemeat add 1 cup finely-chopped fresh pears or apples, sliced orange sections (remove the membranes) or sliced preserved peaches or pineapple. Bake 5-10 minutes longer at 350 degrees. *Serves 8.*

Pear and Mincemeat Pie

sufficient pastry for a two-crust 10" pie
$1/2$ cup chopped fresh walnuts
8-10 Preserved Pear halves (see page 70)
2 cups Pear Mincemeat (see page 73)
2 tablespoons butter
2 tablespoons rum

Sprinkle half the walnuts in the bottom of the pie shell. Slice the pears lengthwise and lay half of them over the nuts. Cover the pears with the mincemeat, make another layer of pears and add the rest of the nuts.

Melt the butter, combine with the rum and pour over the pears. Wet the pastry on the rim of the pie plate with water, cover with the top crust, trim and flute the edges. Slash 6-8 steamholes in the top crust.

Bake at 425 degrees for 10 minutes, reduce the heat to 375 degrees and continue baking 30-40 minutes, or until the crust is golden and the filling is bubbling up.

Serve warm with vanilla ice cream. *Enough for 8 people.*

Pear and Ginger Pie

one 9" unbaked, unpricked pie shell

Topping

$1/3$ cup firmly packed brown sugar
$2/3$ cup sifted all-purpose flour
$1/2$ teaspoon cinnamon
$1/8$ teaspoon ground ginger
$1/4$ cup butter
2 tablespoons chopped candied ginger

Filling

6 medium pears, ripe and juicy
1 teaspoon lemon juice
$1/2$ teaspoon grated lemon rind
$1/3$ cup white sugar
2 tablespoons chopped candied ginger
2 tablespoons heavy cream
1 tablespoon ginger syrup (optional)

For topping, combine the brown sugar, flour and spices. Cut in the butter with a pastry blender. Add the candied ginger.

Peel and core the pears. Divide each into 6 pieces and sprinkle with lemon juice.

Put half of the topping in the pie shell. Arrange the pears attractively in the shell, sprinkle with lemon rind, the white sugar, chopped candied ginger, cream and syrup. Sprinkle on the rest of the topping.

Bake at 425 degrees for 10 minutes. Reduce heat to 350 degrees and bake about 30 minutes, or until the pears are tender and the crust golden brown. *Enough for 6 servings.*

Sour Cream Apple Pie

one 10" unbaked, unpricked pie shell
1 cup sugar, white, brown, grated maple or a
    combination
2 tablespoons flour
1/8 teaspoon salt
1 cup commercial sour cream
4 cups peeled, cored, sliced apples
1 teaspoon cinnamon or 1/2 teaspoon freshly
    grated nutmeg
2 tablespoons brown sugar or grated maple
    sugar

Combine the 1 cup sugar, flour and salt in a bowl. Stir in the cream to make a smooth mixture. Arrange the apples in circles of slices in the pie shell. Spoon the cream mixture evenly over the apples. Sprinkle on the spice and the 2 tablespoons sugar (maple sugar is recommended).

Bake at 425 degrees for 15 minutes, reduce the heat to 350 degrees and continue baking for 35 minutes, or until the apples are tender and the pastry golden brown. *Easily serves 8.*

Olive Davis' Schnitz Peach Pie

I call my mother, Olive Davis, the Pie Queen, because I think she makes the best pies to be found in Canada.

one 10" unbaked, unpricked pie shell
2/3 cup firmly packed brown sugar
3 tablespoons flour
pinch of salt
2 tablespoons butter
6 peeled, halved, stoned peaches
2 teaspoons lemon juice
1/4 cup heavy cream
1/2 teaspoon cinnamon

Combine the sugar, flour and salt. Add the butter and mix until crumbly. Spoon about 1/3 of this mixture into the pie shell.

Cut each peach half into 3 slices and arrange all the slices attractively over the crumbs. Sprinkle on the lemon juice and cream and the rest of the crumbs. Dust on the cinnamon.

Bake at 425 degrees for 10 minutes, reduce the heat to 375 and bake another 30-35 minutes, or until the peaches are tender, and the crust crisp and golden.

Like all peach pies, this one is at its best while still just warm, when the crust is flaky and crisp and the filling gorgeously runny. *Serves 6-8.*

Peach Custard Pie

one deep 9" unbaked, unpricked pie shell
5-6 medium peaches
1/3 cup white sugar
1/4 teaspoon freshly grated nutmeg
1/4 teaspoon cinnamon
2 tablespoons butter
1 egg yolk
1/4 cup medium or heavy cream

Chill the pie shell.

Peel the peaches, stone and cut into eighths. Arrange attractively in the pie shell. Combine the sugar and spices and sprinkle over the pie. Dot with butter.

Bake at 425 degrees for 10 minutes, reduce heat to 350 degrees and cook 20 minutes.

Beat the yolk and cream together. Drizzle evenly over the fruit. Bake 15 minutes more, or until the fruit is tender and the custard set.

Serve within 2-3 hours of when it comes out of the oven. *Enough for 6-8.*

John Clements' Jelly Apple Pie

I was given this recipe at the 1976 Kingston Festival of Canadian Books, where I met John Clements and his wife. In the 1940s, John Clements made pies like this for the Master's Grill which he operated in Hamilton on the site of what is now

Hamilton Place. The pies were so popular that he couldn't keep up with the demand.

It's an uncommon recipe. The double-crust pie is baked with an unsweetened apple filling. All the apple parings and cores are saved, boiled with water and the juice extracted, as for jelly. This juice is rich in acid and pectin and, sweetened with sugar, it is poured under the top crust of the pie as it comes out of the oven. The juice jells and sweetens the pie at the same time. In order to ensure the jelling, use tart fresh apples. I suggest making this pie in the fall, when you can be sure that the apples didn't come out of storage.

> sufficient pastry for a two-crust 9" pie
> 4-5 medium-large apples
> 1 teaspoon lemon juice
> 1/4 teaspoon grated lemon rind
> 2 tablespoons butter
> 1 teaspoon water
> 1 cup water
> 3/4 cup white sugar
> 1/8 teaspoon freshly grated nutmeg

Peel and core the apples, reserving the peelings and cores. Slice the apples so that you have 6 cups of apple. Place the apple slices, lemon juice and rind, butter and 1 teaspoon of water in a heavy-bottomed saucepan with a close-fitting lid. Set over medium-low heat and cook gently for 15 minutes, or until the apples are just tender but have not lost their shape. Cool slightly while you are rolling out the bottom crust.

Line the pie plate with pastry and spoon the apples gently into the bottom crust. Wet the pastry on the rim of the pie plate and cover with the top crust. Trim and flute the edges. With a decorative cutter, cut out a circle about 1 1/2" wide in the centre of the pie.

Bake at 425 degrees for 15 minutes, reduce heat to 375 degrees and cook for another 20 minutes, or until the crust is evenly browned.

In the last 20 minutes of the baking period, combine the peelings, cores and the cup of water in a saucepan. Cover, bring to the boil, reduce the heat and simmer for about 10 minutes, or until the peelings and cores are tender. Press through a sieve, extracting as much of the juice and pulp as possible. Discard the peelings and cores.

Combine the resulting juice, the sugar and the nutmeg in a clean saucepan. Place over high heat and bring to the boil. Boil vigorously for 3-4 minutes. Stir constantly. The juice will thicken and show signs of jelling.

Remove the pie from the oven and, using a funnel if necessary, pour the apple syrup into the hole in the pie. The liquid will be absorbed into the layers of apples and not only sweeten the whole pie, but form a real jelly between the layers.

Allow to cool thoroughly and serve with whipped cream. *Enough for 6 servings.*

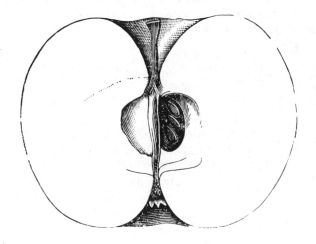

Helen Harris' Upside-Down Apple Pie

In my first cookbook, *Classic Canadian Cooking*, I included a recipe that I remember from my childhood visits to my aunt, Helen Harris. It was an upside-down apple pie, covered with whipped cream. One night while listening to the radio, I heard an old lumber-jack talking about food from the old days in the lumber camps of the Ottawa valley. He described almost the same pie as my aunt's and said it was one of the men's favourites. So I included a recipe for it in the book and named the pie Lumber Camp Apple Pie.

Now when you write a cookbook you get a terrific number of people who try out the recipes and afterwards tell you how they liked them, but so far no one has commented on Lumber Camp Apple Pie. Since it is one of my favourites, I thought that perhaps if the recipe had a new name (just as genuine) and some minor improvements, it might get the attention it deserves.

1 teaspoon butter
6 cups peeled, cored, sliced apples
2/3-3/4 cup white sugar
2 tablespoons flour
pinch of salt
1/4 teaspoon cloves or freshly grated nutmeg
    or 1/2 teaspoon cinnamon
2 tablespoons melted butter
1 tablespoon lemon juice
sufficient pastry to cover a deep 9" or regular
    10" pie plate
1 cup heavy cream
1 teaspoon sugar
1/4 teaspoon vanilla

Use the 1 teaspoon butter to grease the pie plate generously, rim and all.

Place the apples in a bowl. Combine the sugar, flour, salt and spice in another bowl and pour over the apples. Toss gently to coat the slices evenly. Turn into the buttered pie plate, levelling them off slightly higher than the rim. Drizzle the butter and lemon juice over the top.

Roll out the pastry, drape over the apples and trim all around the rim. Flute the pastry along the rim. Make a 1/4" slash in the middle.

Bake at 425 degrees for 10 minutes. Reduce the heat to 350 degrees and bake 45-50 minutes, or until the apples are tender and juicy.

Cool. Loosen the crust around the edges. Place a large flat serving plate over the pie and turn over. Lift off the pie plate carefully.

Whip the cream, add sugar and flavouring. Pipe or spread evenly over the apples. Serve immediately. *Serves 6-8.*

Apple Dumplings or Paddy Bundles

Pastry

2 cups sifted all-purpose flour
4 teaspoons baking powder
1/2 teaspoon salt
1/3 cup butter
2/3 cup milk

Filling

6 medium-large apples
3 tablespoons slivered almonds, raisins or
    diced mixed peel (optional)
6 teaspoons butter
6 tablespoons brown sugar
3/4 teaspoon cinnamon

Sauce

1 cup water
1 cup fresh cider or apple juice
1 1/2 cups firmly packed brown sugar
1/2 teaspoon freshly grated nutmeg
3 tablespoons butter

Sift the flour, baking powder and salt into a large mixing bowl. Using a pastry blender, cut the 1/3 cup butter into the dry ingredients until the mixture has the consistency of rough oatmeal. Add the milk, mixing lightly with a fork as you pour in the milk. Form into a ball. Turn out onto a lightly-floured board and roll out to 3/8" thick. Divide the pastry into 6 even squares.

Peel and core the apples, leaving 1/2" at the bottom of the core to hold the filling. Place an apple in the centre of each square of pastry. In the core of the apple place 1/2 tablespoon of the optional nuts, raisins or peel, 1 teaspoon of butter and 1 tablespoon of sugar. Sprinkle 1/8 teaspoon of the cinnamon over each apple. Moisten the inside of the pastry sparingly, fold up over the apples, covering the entire apple and sealing the edges well. Prick 6 holes in the top with a fork. Place the pastry-wrapped apples in a buttered 9" × 12" ovenproof dish.

Combine the ingredients for the sauce in a medium saucepan. Place over high heat and bring to the boil, stirring to make sure that the sugar has dissolved evenly. Pour around the apples.

Bake at 375 degrees for 45 minutes. Baste the dumplings every 5-10 minutes with the sauce. As the dumplings bake, the sauce bubbles up around them, thickening slightly as the cooking period nears its end. The pastry turns a delicious, crisp, shiny golden brown. At the end of the cooking period, test the doneness of the apple with a skewer inserted through the crust in an inconspicuous place. Return to the oven if the apples are still firm and continue baking until tender.

These apples are best when served hot from the oven with a generous pitcher of medium cream. *Serves 6 lavishly*.

Apple Turnover Deluxe

1 recipe of Standard Pastry (see page 27)
2 cups chopped, peeled and cored apples
1 tablespoon butter
3 tablespoons white wine
1 teaspoon lemon juice
1/3 cup firmly packed brown sugar
1/4 teaspoon mace
1/4 cup raisins
1/4 cup mixed peel
1 egg
1 teaspoon water
2-3 teaspoons white sugar

Combine the apples, butter, wine, lemon juice, brown sugar, mace, raisins and peel in a heavy-bottomed saucepan. Place over medium-low heat and cook covered until the apples are tender. Uncover and cook until the moisture is absorbed. Cool.

Roll out half the pastry so that it is very thin. Cut into 3" squares. Beat together the egg and water and use to paint along the edges of two adjoining sides of each pastry square. Place a spoonful of the apple filling in the middle. Fold the unpainted sides over the filling and press onto the painted edge to form triangles. Crimp the 2 sides with the tines of a fork. Paint the top of each turnover with the egg wash, sprinkle with sugar and cut a neat steam hole in the top crust.

Repeat with the remaining pastry and bake on ungreased baking sheets at 425 degrees for 8 minutes. Reduce the heat to 350 degrees and bake 15-20 minutes longer or until golden on top.

Serve warm with vanilla ice cream. *Yields 30 squares*.

Apple Butter Pie

This is an improved version of the only recipe I have found for an apple butter pie. It's made with apple butter and custard with a grating of nutmeg and orange rind. Apple butter is so rich on its own that it needs the custard.

It is difficult to duplicate the apple butter found in farmers' markets. I have tried many recipes over the years to make that dark, rich, runny stuff, but the best I can do comes out a medium brown and is set rather firm, much like the sort sold in health food stores. I have asked the farmers how they do it, and they assure me it's simple. You just boil down fresh cider, add the cooked applesauce and simmer for several hours. No sugar or spices are needed. I did just that, and although the results were better, it was still not the real McCoy. I suspect their secret is using bruised and windfall apples (or even the slightly rotten apples also used to make cider). I'm going to keep trying, but in the meantime, I'm buying my apple butter.

> one 10" unpricked, unbaked pie shell
> 3 eggs
> 1/2 cup firmly packed brown sugar
> 3/4 cup apple butter
> 1 cup milk
> 1 cup light cream
> pinch of salt
> 1/4-1/2 teaspoon grated orange rind
> 1/4 teaspoon freshly grated nutmeg

Chill the pie shell.

Beat the eggs in a large mixing bowl, add all the ingredients except the nutmeg and beat until well blended. Let the filling rest 10 minutes so that all the bubbles subside.

Pour the filling into the pie shell. Sprinkle the nutmeg over the top. Bake in the lower third of the oven at 450 degrees for 10 minutes. Reduce the heat to 350 degrees and bake another 30-35 minutes, or until a knife inserted in the middle comes out clean.

Cool on a rack. This pie is best when freshly made, just barely warm from the oven. A bowl of whipped cream flavoured with grated orange rind or a teaspoon of orange liqueur goes well with it. *Serves 8.*

August Apple and Peach Pie

> sufficient pastry for a deep, two-crust 9" pie
> 3 cups sliced, peeled and cored apples
> 1 1/2 cups sliced, peeled and stoned peaches
> 2/3 cup seeded or golden sultana raisins (dark seeded raisins have more flavour than the lighter sultanas; your choice depends on your personal preference)
> 2/3 cup firmly packed brown sugar
> 2 tablespoons flour
> 1/8 teaspoon salt
> 1/4 teaspoon freshly grated nutmeg
> 1/2 teaspoon cinnamon
> 1/8 teaspoon allspice
> 1/4 teaspoon mace
> 2 teaspoons lemon juice
> 2 tablespoons butter
> 2 tablespoons red currant jelly, apricot jam, or peach conserve
> 1 teaspoon milk
> 1/2 teaspoon white sugar

Combine the apples, peaches, raisins, brown sugar, flour, salt and spices in a large mixing bowl. Mix lightly but thoroughly. Spoon into the prepared bottom crust, heaping the filling up slightly in the middle. Sprinkle on the lemon juice. Dot with the butter and jelly.

Moisten the pastry on the rim of the pie plate with water, cover with the top crust, trim and flute the edges firmly. Slash 8-10 decorative steam holes around the middle of the top crust. Brush the top crust lightly with the milk and sprinkle with the 1/2 teaspoon white sugar.

Bake at 425 degrees for 15 minutes. Reduce heat to 375 degrees and bake 35-40 minutes. The crust should be a lovely golden brown, and the fruit should be tender. A good way to test the doneness of the filling is to gently insert the tip of a knife through one of the steam holes.

Because of the richness of the filling, this pie is especially good with lightly whipped, unsweetened cream. *Serves 6 generously.*

Apple Cranberry Nut Pie

one 10" unbaked, unpricked pie shell

Filling

> 5 cups peeled, cored, sliced apples
> 1 cup coarsely chopped cranberries
> 1/3 cup sultana raisins
> 1 teaspoon lemon juice or rum
> 2/3 cup white sugar (1/2 cup if you prefer a tart pie)
> 1 1/2 tablespoons flour
> 1/2 teaspoon cinnamon
> 3/4 cup slivered, blanched almonds, fresh, chopped walnuts, or pecans

Crumb Topping

> 1/4 cup cold butter
> 1/2 cup firmly packed brown sugar
> 1/2 cup sifted all-purpose flour

Combine the apples, cranberries and raisins in a bowl. Toss together with the lemon juice. Mix the white sugar, flour and cinnamon together. Pour over the fruit and mix until well distributed. Turn into the pie shell, evening out the top. Sprinkle on the almonds.

Place the butter, brown sugar and flour in a bowl. Cut the butter into the sugar and flour using a pastry blender or 2 knives. The mixture should be crumbly. Spoon evenly over the almonds and fruit filling.

Bake at 425 degrees for 10 minutes. Reduce heat to 350 degrees and continue baking until the pastry is golden, the top crispy and the fruit tender when pierced with the tip of a knife.

Serve while still slightly warm from the oven with a bowl of sour or whipped cream. As this pie is very rich, a little will go a long way. *Serves 8-10.*

Pear and Elderberry Pie

A pie made exclusively of elderberries is too much of a good thing. What's more, since wild fruit is often hard to get in large quantities, it's a fine idea to divide it up, using some for a pie and some for jelly (see page 65). Apples or pears complement elderberries beautifully. They supply the background mellowness and smooth texture to the rich purple colour, crunchy seeds and tart flavour of the elderberry.

> sufficient pastry for a two-crust 9" pie
> 1 1/2 cups peeled, cored, chopped pears
> 2 2/3 cups elderberries, stripped from their
>   stems
> 2/3 cup white sugar
> 2 tablespoons flour
> 1 tablespoon lemon juice

Combine all the ingredients for the filling and spoon into the pie shell. Wet the pastry on the rim of the pie plate, place the top crust over the fruit, press the edges together, trim and flute. As elderberries are very juicy, it is important to be careful with these steps.

Next, cut a circular hole, 1/2"-3/4" in diameter, in the centre of the top crust. Make a small funnel the same diameter as the hole out of aluminum foil. Insert the funnel into the hole. As the juices bubble up, they will be trapped in the funnel, rather than spilling over the crust and onto the oven.

Bake at 425 degrees for 10 minutes, reduce the heat to 350 degrees and bake 30-40 minutes longer, or until the crust is golden and the juices are bubbling up into the funnel. *Serves 6.*

Apple and Elderberry Pie

Proceed as for the Pear and Elderberry Pie, substituting sliced apples for the pears and adding 1/4 teaspoon of mace.

Custard Top Dried Apple Pie

> one deep, unbaked, unpricked 10" pie shell

Filling

> 1/2 pound dried apples (3 cups, packed into a
>   measuring cup)
> 1 3/4 cups water
> 1/4 cup orange juice
> 1/2 teaspoon grated orange rind
> 1/2 teaspoon cinnamon
> 1/4 cup white or firmly packed brown sugar

Custard

> 2 egg yolks
> 1/4 cup white sugar
> 1/8 teaspoon salt
> 3/4 cup milk
> 1/4 cup light cream
> 1/4 teaspoon vanilla
> freshly grated nutmeg

Put the dried apples, water, orange juice and rind into a saucepan. Cover, bring to the boil, reduce heat and simmer until the apples are soft and still moist (about 20 minutes). Stir in the cinnamon and and sugar. Let stand until cool.

Prepare the custard in a mixing bowl. Beat the yolks lightly, stir in the sugar, salt, milk, cream and vanilla.

Spoon the apple mixture into the pie shell and smooth the surface with the back of a spoon. Cover with the custard and grate a sprinkling of nutmeg over the top.

Bake at 425 degrees for 10 minutes. Reduce the heat to 325 degrees and bake 30-40 minutes more, or until the crust is golden brown and the custard is set. Best served when still warm. *Serves 8.*

Peach Apricot Meringue Pie

one 9" unbaked, unpricked pie shell

Filling

> 1/2 cup white sugar
> 1 tablespoon flour
> pinch of salt
> 1 1/2 cups peeled, stoned, sliced peaches
> 1 1/2 cups unpeeled, stoned, sliced apricots
> 1/2 teaspoon grated orange rind
> 1 tablespoon butter, melted
> 1 tablespoon orange juice
> 2 egg yolks

Meringue

> 2 egg whites
> pinch of salt
> 3 tablespoons white sugar
> 1 drop almond extract

Line the pie shell with aluminum foil, fill with rice or dried beans, and bake 10 minutes at 425 degrees. Remove the foil and rice and cool the pie shell.

Combine the dry ingredients for the filling in a large bowl. Add the remaining ingredients for the filling and toss gently to coat the fruit slices evenly. Spoon into the pie shell. Bake at 375 degrees for 30 minutes. After baking, the filling should be set and the pastry golden.

Beat the egg whites and the salt for the meringue at a low speed until frothy. Increase the speed to high and beat until the whites stand in soft peaks. Continue beating, adding the remaining sugar gradually and then the almond extract. A good meringue is glossy and stands in firm but not dry peaks. There is not enough meringue to cover the whole pie, but enough to pipe rosettes all around the edge and in the middle. Return the pie to the oven and bake for another 5 minutes at 375 degrees, or until the meringue is lightly browned. *Serves 6.*

Caramel Apple Pie

This recipe from the West Coast creates a caramel sauce as it bakes around the apples.

> sufficient pastry for a two-crust 10" pie
> 1 cup firmly packed brown sugar
> 1/4 cup flour
> 1/4 teaspoon salt
> 3/4 cup water
> 1 teaspoon cider vinegar
> 2 tablespoons butter
> 1 teaspoon vanilla
> 8 cups peeled, cored, sliced apples
> 1 teaspoon milk
> 1 teaspoon white sugar

Combine the brown sugar, flour and salt in a saucepan. Stir in the water and vinegar, mixing well to prevent lumps. Cook over medium-low heat, stirring constantly until the sauce is thick and smooth (about 4 minutes). Remove from the heat and add the butter and vanilla.

Line the pie plate with pastry, but do not trim. Fill with the apples and pour the caramel sauce over the apples. Wet the pastry on the rim of the pie plate, cover with the top crust, trim and flute. Slash 6 steam holes in the top. Brush the top crust with milk and sprinkle with the white sugar.

Bake at 425 degrees for 15 minutes, reduce the heat to 350 degrees and continue baking for 30 minutes. The slices of apple should be tender (to test, poke with the tip of a paring knife through the steam slits), and the top a beautiful golden brown.

Very good still warm from the oven with vanilla ice cream. *Serves 8.*

Figgy Pear Tarts

According to a family story, whenever a young man came to call on one of my aunts, my grandmother would bake up a making of tarts. She had three specialties — fig and pear, raspberry and lemon curd — all served with whipped cream. The young callers must have been suitably impressed; there are no single women in my family. All of the tarts are delicious, but the fig and pear, with just a taste of cardamom, are the most unusual.

> sufficient pastry for 12 standard tart shells (2³/₄"), about half a making of the pastry (see page 27)

Filling

> ¹/₂ pound dried figs (1¹/₄-1¹/₃ cups loosely placed in a measuring cup)
> 1¹/₂ cups water
> 1¹/₂ cups peeled, cored, finely chopped pears
> ¹/₄ cup white sugar
> ¹/₄ cup orange juice
> ¹/₂ teaspoon grated orange rind
> ¹/₈ teaspoon ground cardamom
> a few grates of nutmeg

Garnish

> 1 cup heavy cream
> 1 teaspoon each of white sugar and rum

Roll the pastry to a thickness of ¹/₄", cut into circles and form neatly into the tart tins. Prick the bottom and sides of each tart with a fork. Bake at 425 degrees for 10-12 minutes or until just lightly browned. Remove from the tins and cool on a rack.

Remove the tough tips from the figs. Soak overnight in a covered saucepan with the water. Bring to the boil over high heat, reduce immediately to low and simmer, still covered, 10 minutes. The figs will be tender but not mushy. Remove the figs with a slotted spoon and let cool on a chopping board. Chop finely when cool enough to handle.

Meanwhile, add the remaining ingredients for the filling to the cooking liquid. Cook uncovered over medium-low heat for 15 minutes. By this time the pears should be translucent. Stir frequently, as the liquid is syrupy and could burn.

Add the chopped figs and continue cooking, stirring occasionally until the sauce has thickened but is neither mushy nor dry. The pears and figs should still retain their shape, and the whole filling will be glossy and a rich bronze brown colour.

Cool and store in a covered container in the refrigerator, if not to be used immediately.

To serve, spoon a generous portion of the filling into the tart shells. Whip the cream, sweeten, flavour with rum and serve over the filling. *Makes 12 tarts.*

Fresh Peach Tarts

> 12 tart shells (see above)
> 3-4 ripe, juicy peaches
> 1 tablespoon peach brandy (optional)
> 2 tablespoons white sugar
> 1 cup heavy cream
> 1-2 tablespoons melted red currant or raspberry jelly (optional)

Peel peaches and divide each one into 8-10 neat slices. Sprinkle on brandy and sugar. Stir gently. Cover and let macerate 1 hour.

Whip the cream. Drain the liquid off the peaches and stir 2 teaspoons into the whipped cream. Pipe or spoon the cream into the tart shells. Top with the peach slices, glaze with a bit of the jelly and serve immediately. *Makes 12 tarts.*

PUDDINGS, ICE CREAMS AND SHERBETS

Thick Unsweetened Applesauce

> 10 medium apples
> $^1/_2$ cup water
> 1 strip of lemon peel, $^1/_2" \times 3"$

Remove the stems and blossom ends from the apples. Wash and cut into eighths. Place in a heavy-bottomed saucepan, add the water and peel and cover tightly. Place over medium-low heat and cook 20-30 minutes, stirring occasionally to prevent the bottom apples from burning. Keep the temperature low and add more liquid if necessary. When the apples are tender, remove from the heat and pass through a sieve, a food mill with a fine disc or a ricer. Discard the cores and peels. *Yields about 2 $^1/_2$ cups thick applesauce.*

Sweetened Applesauce

> 2 $^1/_2$ cups Thick Unsweetened Applesauce
> (see above)
> $^1/_2$-$^2/_3$ cup liquid clover honey or white sugar

Stir the applesauce and sweetening together. Heat slightly if necessary to dissolve the sugar.

Cranberry Applesauce

Follow the procedure for Thick Unsweetened Applesauce, using 9 apples and 1 cup cranberries. Sweeten.

Elderberry or Grape Apple or Pear Sauce

Follow the procedure for Thick Unsweetened Applesauce, using 9 apples or juicy pears and 1 cup elderberries or grapes stripped from their stems. Sweeten.

Honey Pear and Applesauce

> 8 large pears
> 4 large apples
> $^1/_4$-$^1/_3$ cup liquid clover honey

Proceed according to the recipe for Thick Unsweetened Applesauce and sweeten with the honey. *Makes about 5 cups sauce.*

Apple Soufflé

2 tablespoons butter
2 large apples
2 tablespoons maple syrup
3 tablespoons butter
3 tablespoons flour
$1/2$ cup hot milk
$1/4$ cup white sugar
$1/4$ cup Thick Unsweetened Applesauce (see page 41)
1 tablespoon dark rum
4 egg yolks
5 egg whites
pinch of salt
$1/4$ teaspoon cream of tartar
1-2 tablespoons icing sugar

Melt the 2 tablespoons butter in a shallow, wide-bottomed saucepan. Peel the apples, cut into 8 sections and core. Arrange the apples in one layer in the bottom of the saucepan. Drizzle the maple syrup evenly over the apples. Cover and cook over medium heat for 8 minutes, or until the apples are tender. Baste 3-4 times during the cooking process with the butter-maple syrup liquid.

Transfer the apples to the bottom of a well-buttered 8-cup soufflé dish. Arrange evenly and attractively on the bottom of the dish. Pour butter-maple syrup liquid over the apples. Set aside.

Melt the 3 tablespoons butter in a heavy-bottomed saucepan. Stir in the flour, cook over medium-low heat for 3-4 minutes without allowing the flour to colour. If the pan is getting too hot, immediately remove the pan from the heat, wait a few minutes to cool and continue at a lower temperature.

Pour in the hot milk, whisking the mixture as you do in order to prevent lumps. Add the sugar, stir to blend well and cook the sauce over low heat for 5 minutes, or until the sauce is smooth and thickened.

Remove from the heat, beat in the applesauce, rum and the egg yolks, one at a time. Set aside, but do not chill. The mixture will blend into the egg whites best if it is just warm.

Beat the egg whites at low speed in a large bowl. When the whites are foamy, add the salt and cream of tartar. Continue beating at high speed, until the egg whites are glossy and stand in firm but not dry peaks.

Stir one-quarter of the egg whites into the applesauce mixture. Pour this lightened mixture into the remaining egg whites and fold together rapidly but smoothly. Spoon the mixture into the soufflé dish over the apples.

Place on the lowest rack in a 400 degree oven. Immediately reduce the heat to 375 degrees and bake for 35-40 minutes. If a skewer stuck into the middle of the soufflé comes out clean, the soufflé is done. Sprinkle with icing sugar and serve immediately. *Serves 6.*

Apple Float

Apple Float is a delicious, light and easy dessert made by folding beaten egg whites into a smooth applesauce. A similar dessert can be made using puréed peaches, raspberries, strawberries or blueberries. The traditional accompaniment is a pitcher of custard sauce.

Custard Sauce

2 cups milk
$1/4$ cup white sugar
$1/8$ teaspoon salt
4 egg yolks
1 teaspoon vanilla

Meringue

3 egg whites at room temperature
$1/4$ cup white sugar

Fruit

$3/4$ cup Sweetened Applesauce (see page 41)
$1/8$ teaspoon freshly grated nutmeg

To make the custard, combine the milk, sugar and salt in the top of a double boiler. Scald over medium direct heat.

Beat the egg yolks and mix about 1/2 cup of the hot mixture into the yolks, stirring well. Stir back into the rest of the milk and cook over barely simmering water until the custard has thickened enough to coat a spoon (about 4 minutes). Stir constantly during the cooking period. Remove from the heat and add the vanilla. Cool, stirring frequently to prevent a skin from forming. If you are making the sauce in advance, pour a very thin layer of cold milk over the top of the custard and stir in just before serving. Strain through a sieve into a pitcher.

To make the meringue, beat the egg whites until they stand in soft peaks and continue beating, gradually adding the 1/4 cup sugar, until the meringue stands in firm, glossy peaks. Fold into the applesauce and spoon into a glass serving bowl or glasses. Sprinkle on the nutmeg. Serve with the custard sauce. *Makes 4-5 servings.*

Peach Foam

custard sauce (see page 42)
3 peaches
meringue (see page 42)
2 drops almond extract

Prepare the custard as for Apple Float. While it is chilling, peel, chop and stone the peaches. Blend to a fine purée. Set the purée in a fine sieve over a bowl and drain for 5 minutes to remove excess juice.

Prepare the meringue as for Apple Float, then fold in the peach purée and almond extract. Spoon immediately into chilled glass dishes and garnish with a small marigold flower or a sprig of mint. Serve with the custard sauce. *Yields 4-5 servings.*

Trifle

Trifle is part of our Anglo-Scot-Irish tradition. It's a natural for Canada because of our abundance of fruit, rich dairy products and skill in baking. Recipes for trifle have appeared regularly in Canadian cookbooks, but two of the best are found in *The New Galt Cook Book* of 1898. Both feature a velvety smooth applesauce, custard and whipped cream.

The Apple Trifle uses cranberries which introduce an interesting new flavour to the traditional trifle. The sherry-soaked Sponge Cake is optional and is included for those who like a base for their trifle.

Peach Trifle

3 cups sliced peaches
1/3 cup white sugar
1 teaspoon lemon juice
2 tablespoons brandy or peach brandy
1/2 Sponge Cake (see page 18)
custard sauce (see page 42)
1 cup heavy cream

Stir the peaches, sugar, lemon juice and brandy together gently.

Trim the edges off the cake and cut into finger-sized pieces. Line the bottom of an 8-cup dish, preferably glass, with the cake. Spoon on the peaches. Lay a piece of plastic wrap directly over the peaches. Let stand for about an hour at room temperature.

Prepare the custard and gently spoon over the peaches. Whip the cream and pipe or spoon it over the top of the custard. Chill thoroughly before serving. *Serves 6-8.*

Apple Trifle

Applesauce

6 apples
1/2 cup fresh cranberries
1/4 cup water, cider or apple juice
1 teaspoon lemon or orange juice
1 strip of lemon or orange peel, 1/2" × 2"
1/2 cup white sugar or liquid clover honey

Medium-Thick Custard

1 cup milk
1/2 cup light cream
1 tablespoon corn starch
1/4 teaspoon salt
1/3 cup white sugar
2 eggs or 4 egg yolks
1/2 teaspoon vanilla

Cake

one 8" Sponge Cake layer (see page 18)
1/2-3/4 cup medium sherry

Topping

1 cup heavy cream
1/2 teaspoon white sugar
1/8 teaspoon grated lemon or orange rind

Wash the apples, remove the stems and blossom ends and cut into eighths. Combine with the cranberries, water, juice and peel in a heavy-bottomed saucepan with a close fitting lid. Cook gently over medium-low heat until the apples are tender and the cranberries well popped (20 minutes). Pass through the fine disc of a food mill, a ricer or sieve. Sweeten and reserve. There should be about 2 cups of smooth, rosy applesauce.

While the apples are cooking, prepare and cool the custard. Pour the milk and cream into the top of a double boiler. Mix together the corn starch, salt and sugar. Stir into the milk, place over boiling water and cook until the sauce is slightly thickened and the taste of raw cornstarch has disappeared (about 8 minutes).

Beat the eggs. Mix 1/2 cup of the hot mixture into the egg and return to the top of the double boiler, stirring well. Cook over barely simmering water until the custard has thickened (about 4 minutes). Stir constantly after the addition of the eggs. Remove from the heat, add the vanilla and cool over cold water, stirring periodically to prevent a skin from forming. Strain and reserve.

To assemble, trim the edges off the cake so that it will fit comfortably into the bottom of your serving bowl. I recommend using a glass soufflé bowl or other glass bowl, so that you can see the layers. Slice the cake horizontally and place one layer in the bowl. Sprinkle on half the sherry. Spoon in half the applesauce, half the custard, the second layer of cake, the rest of the sherry, applesauce and custard. Cover well and, if possible, refrigerate for 24 hours to mellow the flavours and soften the cake.

To serve, whip the cream, stir in the 1/2 teaspoon sugar and grated rind. Spoon or pipe attractively over the top of the custard. *Makes 8-10 servings.*

Note: There is an easier trifle which consists of the applesauce (no cranberries), custard layers and the whipped cream. Proceed as with the recipe above, but do not use the sherried cake. This simple trifle is exquisitely smooth and creamy and recommended when you have superbly flavoured apples, such as Wealthy, Red Astrachan, Duchess or fresh Northern Spy Apples.

Mrs. Beeton's Stewed Pears in Port

Mrs. Beeton, a mid-nineteenth century English cookbook writer, had considerable influence on Canadian cooking, especially among the more well-to-do Canadians of English ancestry. Copies and variations of recipes that can be traced back to her book, *Beeton's Book of Household Management*, appeared frequently, especially in personal hand-written recipe collections.

$^1/_2$ cup white sugar
1 cup port
2 cups water
6 medium-large pears, ripe but firm
6 whole cloves
4 allspice berries

Combine the sugar, port and water in a saucepan just large enough to hold the pears in one layer. Bring to the boil. Peel the pears, but leave them on the stem. Stick a clove in each pear and put in the saucepan along with the allspice berries. Bring back to the boil, reduce the heat and simmer over very low heat for about $2^1/_2$ hours, or until the pears are tender, dark rich red in colour and translucent. Turn the pears carefully 3-4 times during the cooking period, and baste frequently with a bulb baster.

Remove the pears and place in serving bowl (a glass dish or shallow bowl is ideal). Cool and strain the cooking liquid over the pears. Serve chilled with unsweetened whipped cream. *Enough for 6.*

Dried Apple and Prune Compote

Dried apples and prunes go well together, especially when they're sweetened with honey and cooked with a handful of raisins and sliced oranges. Served with a bowl of sour cream dusted with mace, this recipe makes a delicious dessert: by itself, it's a simple, but good breakfast dish.

$^3/_4$ pound prunes (2 cups)
1 cup dried apples
$^2/_3$ cup sultana raisins
$^1/_2$ orange, thinly sliced
3 cups cold water
$^1/_3$ cup honey or white or firmly packed
    brown sugar

Combine the first 5 ingredients in a saucepan and soak overnight.

Add the honey, cover and bring to the boil over high heat. Reduce the heat to low and simmer gently 15 minutes. Cool.

Store in the refrigerator. *Makes 6-8 servings.*

Simple Baked Apples

6 medium-large apples
$^2/_3$ cup raisins or chopped almonds
$^2/_3$ cup firmly packed brown sugar
3 tablespoons butter
$^1/_2$ teaspoon grated lemon or orange rind
$1^1/_2$ cups water

Wash and core the apples, leaving about $^1/_2$" of apple at the bottom to hold the filling. About two-thirds of the way up each apple, make a shallow cut in the skin all around the apple. This cut allows the apple to expand during the cooking process.

Fill the cored apples with the raisins. Place the apples in a shallow, heatproof dish large enough to accommodate them without touching.

Combine the remaining ingredients in a saucepan and heat just long enough to dissolve the sugar and melt the butter. Pour over and around the apples.

Bake at 375 degrees for about 30-45 minutes, or until the apples are tender. Baste frequently with the brown sugar sauce.

Serve with unsweetened lightly whipped cream. *Enough for 6.*

Maple Baked Apples

Proceed according to the Simple Baked Apples, using the almonds and substituting 1 cup maple syrup for the brown sugar and water syrup. Grate a little nutmeg over the top of the apples before baking.

Mincemeat Baked Apples

Proceed according to Simple Baked Apples, substituting 2/3-3/4 cup Rich Mincemeat (see page 72) for the raisin filling.

Nut-Meringue Maple Baked Apples

Make the Maple Baked Apples, and 5 minutes before the end of the baking time, prepare a meringue as for Apple Meringue Cake (see page 12). Pipe or spoon the meringue over the top of the apples. Increase the heat in the oven to 425 degrees, and bake for 4-5 minutes, or until the meringue is golden.

Oven Baked Pears

Baked Pears may sound boring, but you'll be pleasantly surprised to discover how nice they look and taste. The slow cooking in a covered container (several old recipes recommended brown crocks) makes them very juicy, slightly pink coloured and lovely tasting.

> 6 ripe but firm pears
> 1/2 cup white sugar
> 1/4 teaspoon freshly grated nutmeg or lemon
>   rind
> 1 teaspoon lemon juice
> 1/3 cup water or white wine
> custard sauce (see page 42)

Peel the pears, cut them in half and neatly remove the seeds and the strings from the stem. Place half of the pears in the bottom of a heatproof dish and sprinkle on half the sugar and nutmeg. Add the remaining pears, sugar, nutmeg, all the lemon juice and water. Cover tightly with a lid or aluminum foil.

Bake at 325 degrees for 2 hours. Remove from the oven and cool on a rack without opening.

When at room temperature, chill thoroughly and serve with custard.

These pears look attractive when served in glasses or glass dishes. *Serves 6.*

Baked Peaches with Slivered Almonds

> 6 medium peaches
> 1/3 cup butter
> 1/4 cup lemon juice
> 1/4 cup orange liqueur
> 1/2 teaspoon grated orange rind
> 3/4 cup firmly packed brown sugar
> 1/2 cup slivered, blanched almonds

Peel, halve and stone the peaches. Place the peach halves cut side up in a shallow, buttered heatproof dish. Melt the butter and combine with the lemon juice, orange liqueur and rind. Pour evenly over the peaches. Sprinkle on the brown sugar and the almonds.

Bake at 375 degrees for 25 minutes. The peaches should be tender, but retain their shape and fresh flavour.

Serve with unsweetened whipped cream or vanilla ice cream. *Enough for 6 servings.*

Fresh Peach Mould

Artificially-flavoured and coloured jelly powder has made gelatine into something that's best suited for a child's dessert. But in the days before these florescent colours and phony flavours, Canadian cooks used a number of gelatine recipes to bring out the real flavour of the fruit. Fresh Peach Mould is one of these. It tastes wonderful any time, but is especially good at the end of an outdoors summer dinner.

> 1 cup white sugar
> 1 1/3 cups water
> 3 strips of orange rind, 1/2" × 3"

1 tablespoon unflavoured gelatine (1
    envelope)
1/4 cup orange juice
6-7 peaches
1/4 teaspoon almond extract
1 tablespoon peach brandy or orange
    flavoured liqueur

Garnish

    3/4 cup heavy cream
    1/2 cup toasted almond flakes
    extra peaches if desired

Combine the white sugar, water and the orange strips in a saucepan. Bring to the boil and boil vigorously for 3 minutes. Remove from the heat.

Stir the gelatine into the orange juice to soften. Add to the hot syrup and mix to dissolve com-pletely. Remove the orange peel.

Peel, stone and blend enough of the peaches to make 2 cups of smooth peach purée. Add with the almond extract and liqueur to the syrup and chill until beginning to set.

Peel and stone the remaining peaches and slice neatly. Attractively line the bottom of a rinsed 5-cup mould with these slices and add just enough of the gelatine mixture to cover them. Chill a few minutes until the peaches are set in place by the gelatine, then add the remaining gelatine.

Chill at least 4 hours, overnight if possible. To serve, unmould (see instructions for Moulded Pears in Port), whip the cream and pipe around the edges. Sprinkle toasted almonds over the cream. Garnish with the extra peaches, if desired. *Serves 8.*

Moulded Pears in Port

Port was a popular Victorian drink, and found its way into the poaching liquid for many fruit recipes. Its colour and flavour combine delightfully with pears. For variety, substitute a medium to sweet white wine.

> 4 medium-large pears
> 1/3-1/2 cup white sugar
> 1 cup water
> 4 whole cloves
> one 1"-piece of cinnamon stick, broken up
> a strip of lemon peel, 1/2" × 2"
> 1 tablespoon gelatine (1 envelope)
> 1/4 cup water or cooled pear liquid, if available
> 1 1/2 tablespoons lemon juice
> 1/2 cup port or medium-sweet white wine
> 1 cup heavy cream, whipped

Peel, core and quarter the pears. Place in a saucepan or ovenproof dish with a tight-fitting lid. Combine the sugar, the cup of water, spices and peel in a saucepan. Heat just enough to dissolve the sugar. Pour over the pears. Cover tightly and bake at 300 degrees for 1 1/4 hours or until tender but not mushy.

Remove the pears carefully and drain on paper towelling. Strain the liquid in which the pears cooked and measure 1 cup into a clean saucepan. If there is another 1/4 cup, use it to soften the gelatine; if not, stir the gelatine into the 1/4 cup water and let stand 3-4 minutes while you heat the pear liquid.

Add the lemon juice and port to the pear liquid and bring to the boil. Remove from the heat and add the softened gelatine, stirring until the gelatine has dissolved completely. Cool over a basin of cold icy water, stirring frequently to speed up the process.

Place the pears decoratively over the bottom and along the sides of a rinsed out 4-cup mould (a fluted mould helps hold the pears upright in place). Pour on the cooled port liquid and chill in the refrigerator 3-4 hours or until set. It helps to push the pears down into the liquid once or twice as the liquid jells. It is also wise to cover the surface of the firm gelatine with plastic wrap if you are keeping it 2-3 days.

To unmould, turn over on the centre of the serving plate. Rinse a clean tea towel in warm water, wring out and wrap around the mould. Remove the towel after 10 seconds. Pick up the mould and plate firmly in both hands, lift up, and jerk both down. The heat and the jerking action should release the moulded pears, but if not, repeat. Lift off the mould, tidy up the plate if necessary and garnish with whipped cream. *Serves 6.*

Fresh Apple Cider and Cranberry Jelly

Fresh cider rapidly turns into hard cider or vinegar. In the past, if cider-drinkers wanted fresh apple cider for the winter, they had two choices. They could keep crushing the apples as needed or, since this was not always practical, they could boil and bottle it. The latter method was common, especially among temperance-minded Canadians. This recipe for cider jelly comes from the bottling tradition. Boiling down the cider not only preserves the cider, but has the added advantage of intensifying the apple flavour.

> 1 1/2 cups fresh cider
> 1 tablespoon gelatine (1 envelope)
> 1/4 cup fresh cider
> 1/4 cup white sugar
> 1 cup sweetened cranberry juice (see page 85)
> 2 teaspoons strained orange juice
> 1 1/2 teaspoons strained lemon juice

Pour the 1 1/2 cups cider into a saucepan. Bring to the boil and boil vigorously for 3 minutes.

Mix the gelatine into the 1/4 cup of cider to

soften. Add the gelatine and sugar to the hot cider, stirring to dissolve completely. Add the remaining juices and cool.

Pour into a rinsed 3-cup mould or glass dish and chill until firm. Unmould and serve with whipped cream flavoured with apple brandy or ¼ teaspoon grated orange rind. *Serves 4-5.*

Peach Velvet

Peach Velvet is a Victorian "company best" kind of dessert, light but rich and creamy with a smooth silk-velvet texture. In fact, "velvet" was a popular name for the recipes which we now call "Bavarians" — a combination of custard, gelatine, flavouring or puréed fruit and whipped cream. If possible, serve this dessert in a pressed or cut glass compote dish.

> 2 cups milk
> ½ cup white sugar
> pinch of salt
> 1 whole egg
> 2 egg yolks
> ¼ teaspoon almond extract
> 2 tablespoons unflavoured gelatine (2
>   envelopes)
> ¼ cup cold water
> 3-4 peaches
> 1 cup heavy cream
> 1 tablespoon peach brandy or orange liqueur
> additional heavy cream
> fresh mint leaves or scented geranium leaves

Heat to scalding the milk, sugar and salt in the top of the double boiler over direct moderate heat. Whisk the whole egg and the yolks in a bowl. Pour about half a cup of the hot milk over them, whisking constantly. Next beat the contents of the bowl into the remaining milk in the top of the double boiler. Place over lightly boiling water. Cook, stirring almost constantly, until the custard is thick enough to coat a spoon. Remove from the heat and stir in the almond extract.

Stir the gelatine into the cold water to soften. Add to the custard and mix until dissolved. Cool, stirring from time to time. The best way of doing this is to place the top of the double boiler in the sink. Run cold water into the sink until it comes half way up the sides of the saucepan. You may want to add a tray of ice cubes to further chill the water. I find it faster to chill a custard in icy water than in the refrigerator.

When the custard is cold and has begun to jell, peel and stone the peaches. Blend or sieve enough to make 2 cups of purée. Stir the peaches and the brandy into the custard. Chill in the refrigerator until it begins to jell again. Whip the cream and fold evenly into the peach custard. Turn into a 6-cup glass compote or mould, rinsed in water. Chill 4 hours minimum, overnight if possible. It is advisable to eat this pudding within 24 hours of its making.

To unmould, see page 48. Decorate with piped rosettes of whipped cream and fresh mint or scented geranium leaves. *Serves 6-8.*

Apple Ginger Ice Cream

Sometimes it's a lot of bother to hand churn ice cream. Good homemade ice cream can also be made in the freezer compartment of a refrigerator. To do so, whip heavy cream and fold beaten egg white into the mixture to keep the texture light. Natural sherbets and ice creams, whether hand churned or frozen in the freezer, do not keep their creamy smoothness and rich, true flavour for more than 2-3 days. But don't worry, you won't have any trouble finishing up this ice cream quickly.

1 cup white sugar
1 cup water
3 strips of lemon peel, $1/2" \times 3"$
$1/4$ cup chopped preserved ginger
5 cups peeled, cored, thinly sliced apples
1 tablespoon lemon juice
$1/8$ teaspoon salt
pinch of cream of tartar
1 egg white
1 cup heavy cream

Combine the first 4 ingredients in a saucepan, bring to the boil and boil 3 minutes. Add the apples, bring back to the boil, then reduce the heat so the mixture bubbles gently. Cook uncovered until the apples are tender (about 15-20 minutes). Remove the ginger and rind and chop. Purée the apples. Combine the chopped ingredients, the apple purée and the lemon juice.

Pour into a 8" x 8" cake pan and freeze uncovered until frozen around the edges and firm but still mushy in the centre (about 45-60 minutes).

Sprinkle the salt and cream of tartar onto the egg white. Beat at low speed until frothy and then increase the speed to high and beat until the egg white stands in firm peaks.

Place the apple mixture into a chilled mixing bowl and beat until creamy coloured, fluffy and smooth. Whip the cream until firm. Fold the cream and egg white into the apple mixture. Pour into a container, lay a piece of plastic wrap directly over the ice cream, cover and freeze until firm (about 3 hours).

This is delicious frozen, but also very good when the apple, cream and meringue have just been combined. Serve in chilled glasses with a garnish of chopped, preserved ginger. *Serves 6.*

Peach Ice Cream

This is the ultimate in peach ice creams. The recipe comes from *The Canadian Home Cook Book*, published in 1877, which is one of the first Canadian examples of a collective effort. The recipes are said to have been "Compiled by Ladies of Toronto and Chief Cities in Canada." Although some of the book's recipes for meat dishes and salads wouldn't appeal to us today, the fruit sherbets and ice creams taste as good in 1977 as they must have 100 years ago.

3 cups fresh peach purée
2 tablespoons orange juice
$1/4$ teaspoon grated orange rind
2 tablespoons peach brandy (optional)
$1 1/2$ cups white sugar
$2 1/2$ cups heavy cream

Combine the peaches, juice, rind, brandy and sugar in a bowl. Cover and let stand for 1 hour at room temperature. Add the cream.

Pour the peach and cream mixture into the can of a churn freezer. Pack crushed ice and coarse salt around the can, in the proportions of 3 parts ice to 1 part salt. Cover, attach the crank and turn the handle steadily but slowly for about 12-15 minutes. As the handle becomes harder to turn, increase the speed. Drain off any melted water and replenish the ice and salt during the churning period to maintain the level.

Remove the can from the churn, carefully wipe off the salty water, open and remove the blades. Either pack the ice cream down into the can or use it as a freezer container for storing the ice cream until serving time. The ice cream can be served immediately. *Makes about 1½ quarts of ice cream.*

Sherbets

Water ices and sherbets are really easy to make in the freezer. The only remotely tricky part is to catch the sweetened fruit purée before it's frozen too hard the first time. I recommend doing the initial freezing in an 8″ x 8″ or 9″ x 9″ cake tin. When the purée is frozen in a 2″ border around the edges of the pan, and the centre is mushy-frozen, it's ready to be beaten. Turn the purée into a well-chilled mixing bowl and beat 2-3 minutes with an electric mixer. It is always a pleasure to see the lumpy, icy mixture turn into a creamy, smooth sherbet. The Pear Ice Water is especially delightful, as it turns a beautiful light golden colour.

After the initial freezing, the sherbet should be packed into an air tight container and refrozen. All frozen fruit ices are easier to serve and to eat if served before they freeze too hard the second time.

Apple Honey Sherbet

2½ cups Thick Unsweetened Applesauce
   (see page 41)
⅓ cup liquid honey
⅓ cup white sugar
1 tablespoon lemon juice
½ teaspoon grated lemon or orange rind
⅛ teaspoon cinnamon
2 egg whites
⅛ teaspoon salt
pinch of cream of tartar
1 tablespoon apple brandy or rum

Combine the applesauce, honey, sugar, juice, rind and cinnamon in a saucepan. Heat and stir only until the sugar has dissolved. Cool, pour into a 9″ x 9″ cake tin or similar container and freeze until mushy (about 1 hour). Remove from the freezer and beat in a chilled bowl with an electric mixer until creamy coloured and smooth. Keep cold while preparing the next step.

Beat the egg whites at low speed until foamy, sprinkle on the salt and cream of tartar, increase speed to high and beat until they stand in firm glossy peaks. Fold with the brandy into the applesauce mixture. Turn into a freezer container, place a piece of plastic wrap directly over the sherbet, cover and freeze until firm but not hard (about 2-3 hours).

Very good combined with vanilla ice cream and served with lacy cookies. *Enough for 6-8 servings.*

Fresh Peach Ice Water

1 cup water
1 cup white sugar
2 strips of lemon peel, $\frac{1}{2}$" × 2"
$3\frac{3}{4}$ cups purée of peaches (6-7 peaches)
$\frac{1}{4}$ cup orange juice
1 teaspoon orange flower water or orange
    liqueur

Garnish (optional)

3 cups sliced peaches
2 tablespoons orange liqueur, rum or brandy
$\frac{1}{3}$ cup chopped pistachio nuts (optional)

Boil the water, sugar and lemon peel for 4 minutes. Cool and remove the peel. Combine with the peaches, orange juice and the 1 teaspoon flavoring. Pour into a 9" x 9" cake pan and place in the freezer. When the mixture is frozen around the edges and mushy in the middle, turn into a chilled mixing bowl and beat until creamy, opaque and a pale pinky-white. Pour into a 5-6 cup container or mould, cover the surface of the ice water with a piece of plastic wrap and then cover the container. Freeze until firm but not too hard.

Meanwhile, soak the sliced peaches in the liqueur. Cover and chill.

Serve scoops of the peach ice water alone in glass dishes or with a few slices of fresh peaches and a sprinkle of pistachio nuts.

If the ice water has been frozen in a mould, remove from the freezer, wrap the bottom and sides in a towel which has been rinsed in warm water and wrung out and turn onto a chilled serving platter. Surround the ice water with peaches and sprinkle with the nuts. *Serves 8.*

Pear Ice Water

1 cup sugar
2 cups water
3 strips of lemon peel, $\frac{1}{2}$" × 2"
1" piece of vanilla bean, pounded

1" cinnamon stick, broken into 2-3 pieces
5 cups chopped pears
2 tablespoons lemon juice
2 tablespoons pear brandy (optional)

Combine the first 5 ingredients in a saucepan. Bring to the boil and boil hard uncovered for 3 minutes. Add the pears, bring back to the boil and reduce the heat so that the pears simmer until tender (about 15-20 minutes depending on the pears). Remove the peel, vanilla bean, and cinnamon.

Blend the pears, or press through a sieve or food mill with a fine disc. Combine with the lemon juice and brandy.

Pour into a 9" x 9" cake tin, freeze until frozen around the edges of the pan and firm but still mushy in the middle. Turn into a chilled bowl and beat with an electric mixer until the frozen pear sauce becomes creamy and smooth. Spoon into a container, lay a piece of plastic wrap directly over the water ice and cover. Freeze until firm. Best when not too hard, spooned into chilled glasses and served with a sprig of mint or a leaf of basil. *Yields about 6 servings.*

Peaches and Ice Cream in Almond Meringues

4 cups sliced peaches
3 tablespoons white sugar
2 tablespoons peach brandy, rum or brandy
1 making Almond Meringue shells (see
    page 53)
1 pint rich vanilla ice cream

Place the peaches, sugar and brandy in a bowl, stir very gently, cover and let stand 1 hour so the flavours can mellow and the juices form.

To serve, place 1 meringue shell on each dessert plate, fill with a scoop of ice cream, and spoon peaches and juice over the top. *Yields 10 servings.*

Almond Meringues

4 egg whites (1/2 cup), at room temperature
1/8 teaspoon salt
1/4 teaspoon cream of tartar
1 cup white sugar
1 teaspoon vanilla or 1/2 teaspoon almond
    extract
1/2 cup finely chopped blanched almonds

Place the egg whites, salt and cream of tartar in a clean mixing bowl. Beat at low speed until the eggs become frothy. Increase the speed and beat until the egg whites stand in firm but not dry peaks. Continue beating, adding the sugar gradually. By the time the sugar is added, the egg white should be glossy and firm. Fold in the vanilla and the almonds.

Line a large baking sheet with aluminum foil. Fill a large piping bag with the meringue and pipe ten to twelve 3"-meringue shells onto the foil. If no piping bag is available, form the meringue shells with a dessert spoon.

For light-coloured, crisp meringue shells the most effective way of baking is to place the shells in an oven set at 150 degrees. Open the door slightly, as for broiling, and leave 10 hours or overnight. Cool. Remove from the foil and store in an airtight container. Meringue shells can be stored for 2 weeks without going stale.

Honey Deluxe Apple Crisp

6 cups sliced, tart apples
1/3 cup liquid honey or sugar (white, maple
    or brown)
1 tablespoon lemon juice
1/2 teaspoon cinnamon
1/8 teaspoon cloves or freshly grated nutmeg
1/4 cup all-purpose flour
1/2 cup rolled oats
2/3 cup firmly packed brown sugar
1/8 teaspoon salt
1/3 cup butter
1/4 cup finely chopped nuts (fresh walnuts,
    butternuts, almonds)

Combine the apples, honey, lemon juice and spices. Toss lightly to distribute the flavours and place in a well-buttered ovenproof dish.

Mix the flour, rolled oats, brown sugar and salt. Cut in the butter until the mixture is crumbly. Stir in the nuts. Sprinkle evenly over the apples.

Bake at 350 degrees for 45 minutes, or until the top is crisp and the apples tender. Delicious still warm from the oven with sour cream, lightly whipped cream, vanilla ice cream or custard sauce (see page 42). *Serves 6.*

Apple Charlotte

Apple Charlotte has been a popular dish for at least 125 years. The recipe for it in the 1861 *Canadian Housewife's Manual of Cookery* called Soyer's Apple Cake is "glazed with a red hot shovel" and "blazed with some rum." Hot work! Not all of the recipes were as exotic, but all were essentially the same, involving a buttered bread case around applesauce so thick and rich that it's almost apple butter. When baked, the case becomes golden and crusty, and the interior firm enough to hold its shape. A very effective dessert turned out on a serving plate and accompanied by a bowl of lightly-whipped cream.

> 7-8 medium apples
> 1 tablespoon butter
> 1 strip of lemon peel, 1/2" × 2"
> 1/4 cup fresh orange juice or cider
> 1/3 cup white sugar
> 2 tablespoons apricot or quince jam or
>   marmalade
> 1 teaspoon vanilla
> 10 thin slices (1/4") of slightly stale,
>   homemade-style white bread
> 1/4 cup butter

Peel, core and slice the apples in thin wedges (7 cups). Melt the 1 tablespoon butter in a heavy-bottomed saucepan. Add the apple slices, lemon peel and orange juice. Cover and cook over low heat for 40 minutes, or until the apples are soft and mushy. Stir frequently, being careful not to let the apples burn. Remove the lemon strip. Mash thoroughly.

Add the sugar and jam. Stirring constantly, continue cooking uncovered over medium heat for 30-40 minutes, until the mixture thickens, and the quantity has been reduced by one-third. Remove from the heat and stir in the vanilla. There should be 2 cups of purée.

Slice the crusts from the bread. Cut 8 of the slices into strips 1" wide. Melt the 1/4 cup butter in a frying pan and lightly dip each side of the slices in the butter (you may need more butter, but do not soak the bread). Line the edges of a 4-cup, straight-sided ovenproof dish with the bread slices. They should overlap slightly, and the long sides should be perpendicular to the bottom. Cut a piece of bread to fit the bottom of the dish, dip it in the butter and place it in the bottom of the dish. Fill the lined dish with the apple purée. Cut the last slice of bread to fit over the apple purée, dip it in the butter and press into place. The bread slices should form a buttery, overlapping case for the apple purée.

Bake at 375 degrees for 35 minutes or until the bread becomes crisp and golden.

Let stand 20-30 minutes after removing from the oven. Turn out onto a flat plate and serve warm with unsweetened, lightly-whipped cream. *Makes 6 servings.*

Apple Betty

> 2 1/4 cups fine, fresh breadcrumbs (crusts and
>   all of homemade-style white bread)
> 1/3 cup melted butter
> 3 cups peeled, cored, thinly sliced apples
> 1/2 cup firmly packed brown sugar
> 1/4 teaspoon freshly grated nutmeg
> 1/4 teaspoon cinnamon
> 1 teaspoon grated lemon rind
> 2 tablespoons lemon juice
> 1/4 cup water

Mix together the crumbs and melted butter. Spread about one-quarter of the buttered crumbs on the bottom of a well-buttered, 1 quart ovenproof dish.

Combine the apples, sugar, spices and lemon rind. Spread half the mixture over the crumbs, add another quarter of the crumbs and the rest of the apples. Sprinkle the lemon juice and water over the top evenly.

Spread the remaining crumbs over the top. Cover (with aluminum foil if there is no lid for the dish) and bake at 350 degrees for 30 minutes.

Remove the cover and cook 20 minutes longer, or until the apples are tender and the crumbs crisp.

Serve hot or warm with plenty of medium cream or custard sauce (see page 42). *Serves 6.*

Note: To make Ginger Apple Betty, add ¼ cup chopped, preserved ginger to the apples instead of the lemon rind. Substitute 1 tablespoon ginger syrup for 1 of the tablespoons of lemon juice.

Swedish Apple Pudding

A Scandinavian influence is obvious in this dessert. Its layers of buttered crumbs and sliced apples are unmoulded and served cold with a glaze of red or black currant jelly and, of course, whipped cream. Taletha M. Carlson contributed this recipe many years ago to the United Farm Wives of Alberta *Cookbook*.

> 2 cups fine fresh breadcrumbs (use only good homemade or homemade-style bread and do not hesitate to use the crusts)
> ½ cup white sugar
> 1 teaspoon cinnamon
> ¼ cup melted butter
> 2 cups Thick Unsweetened Applesauce (see page 41)
> ½ cup red or black currant jelly
> 1 cup heavy cream

Combine the crumbs, sugar and cinnamon in a bowl. Mix in the butter. Butter a 4-cup ovenproof bowl (an English-type steamed pudding dish, a soufflé or Charlotte mould are ideal). Place about one-fifth of the crumbs over the bottom of the bowl and up the sides to a height of about 1". Spoon in about one-quarter of the applesauce, being sure not to extend it above the crumbs. Cover the applesauce with a second layer of crumbs, building up the edges again around the sides of the bowl. Continue the layers of sauce and crumbs, finishing with the crumbs. Pat down gently with the back of a spoon.

Bake at 375 degrees for 30-35 minutes, or until the crumbs are nicely browned. Remove from the oven and cool in the baking bowl.

To serve, melt the jelly over medium-low heat. Invert the pudding onto a flat plate and pour the jelly over the top, letting it cover the sides evenly and attractively. Whip the cream and serve it separately. *Serves 6.*

Stale cake or cookie crumbs (mild vanilla type) may be substituted for up to 1 cup of the breadcrumbs. Reduce the sugar to ⅓ cup.

Bird's Nest Pudding

Bird's Nest Pudding evokes the pioneer period, partly because of the homespun quality of its name, and partly because it is a simple dish composed of apples and custard baked together. And the cored baked apples *do* look like bird's nests! This recipe dates back to the days of outdoor bake ovens and brick chimney ovens, when fires were lit in the ovens and left to die out. Then when the ashes were raked out, breads and pies were put in on long wooden paddles and baked while the oven was at its hottest. After those important staples came cookies and cakes, and then in a cooler oven — in fact, just right for custard — in went the Bird's Nest Pudding.

8 medium-sized sweet apples
1/2 teaspoon grated lemon rind
1 cup firmly packed brown sugar
2 tablespoons butter

Custard

5 eggs, well beaten
2 1/2 cups milk
1/2 cup white sugar
1 teaspoon vanilla or rum
1/2 teaspoon freshly grated nutmeg or 1
  teaspoon cinnamon
2 tablespoons white sugar

Butter a shallow ovenproof dish big enough to accommodate the apples in one layer. Core the apples, leaving 1/2" at the bottom to hold the filling. In each apple, put a bit of lemon rind, 2 tablespoons of the brown sugar and a dot of butter.

Place apples in the buttered dish and bake in a 350 degree oven for 30-35 minutes, until the apples are almost cooked. Remove from oven.

Whisk the eggs in a large bowl. Add the milk, 1/2 cup sugar and the flavouring. Combine well.

Strain the custard around the apples and into the cores. Sprinkle the nutmeg or cinnamon on the top.

Return to the oven and bake at 325 degrees for about 20 minutes until the custard is just set and the apples are well cooked.

Cool. Sprinkle with the 2 tablespoons white sugar and serve. *Serves 8.*

Meringue of Pears

2/3 cup white sugar
1 1/2 cups water
1" piece of vanilla bean, pounded
3 thin slices of orange
6 ripe but firm large pears
1 tablespoon lemon juice
1 tablespoon pear brandy (optional)

Meringue

3 egg whites
1/8 teaspoon salt
pinch of cream of tartar
1/3 cup white sugar
1/2 teaspoon vanilla
1/3 cup slivered or sliced almonds

Combine the sugar, water, vanilla bean and orange slices in a saucepan. Bring to the boil and boil for 3 minutes.

Peel, core and slice the pears. Add to the liquid and poach gently uncovered until tender (about 15-20 minutes). Remove the vanilla bean and orange slices and discard. With a slotted spoon remove the pear slices and place in an ovenproof dish (a glass soufflé dish is ideal).

Boil the poaching liquid until reduced to about 1 cup. Remove from the heat and add the lemon juice and brandy. Pour over the pears.

To make the meringue, beat the egg whites at slow speed until foamy. Sprinkle on the salt and cream of tartar. Beat until they stand in soft peaks. Continue beating, gradually adding the sugar and the vanilla until the meringue stands up in firm, glossy peaks.

Pipe or spread the meringue over the pears.

Sprinkle on the nuts and bake at 425 degrees for 4-5 minutes or until lightly browned.

Best while still warm accompanied by a custard sauce (see page 42). *Serves 6-8.*

Apple Custard Meringue

6-8 medium apples
1/4 teaspoon grated lemon or orange rind
    (optional)
1/2 cup water
1/2 cup white sugar or honey
3/4 cup light cream
2 tablespoons white sugar
3 eggs, separated
1/2 teaspoon rum, brandy or vanilla
3 tablespoons white sugar

Wash the apples. Remove the stems and blossom ends. Quarter and place in a saucepan with the rind and water. Cover and bring to the boil over high heat. Reduce the heat and cook until the apples are tender (about 10 minutes, depending on the variety).

Remove from the heat and press through a sieve, ricer or the fine disc of a food mill.

Return the apple purée to a clean saucepan. Cook over medium-low heat, stirring almost constantly until most of the water has evaporated. Add the half cup of sweetening and continue cooking and stirring until the sauce is thick and smooth. Taste and add more sweetening if desired. This takes about 30 minutes in all. Remove from the heat and reserve.

Scald the cream and the 2 tablespoons of sugar together in the top of a double boiler over direct heat. Pour about half of the hot cream into the egg yolks, whisking as you do so. Return the cream-yolk mixture to the top of the double boiler. Mix well. Place over simmering water and cook, stirring constantly, until the custard is thick enough to coat a spoon (about 5 minutes). Remove from the heat immediately to prevent curdling.

Butter a 6-8 cup soufflé dish or heatproof baking dish. Make a ring around the edge of the dish with the apple sauce. Spoon the custard into the middle. At this point it is possible to proceed with the pudding or keep it chilled until just before serving when all that is necessary is to add the meringue and bake.

Beat the egg whites until they form soft peaks. Gradually add 2 1/2 of the 3 tablespoons of sugar and the rum. Continue beating until the peaks are stiff but not dry. Pipe or spread this meringue gently over the entire surface of the applesauce and custard. If you do not have a piping bag, smooth out the meringue and make a ripple pattern with a fork. Sprinkle on the remaining sugar.

Bake at 350 degrees for 15 minutes or until golden brown. Serve hot from the oven or warm. *Enough for 6 generous servings.*

Meringue Apple Pudding

1/4 cup butter
1/2 cup firmly packed brown sugar
1/4 cup white sugar
8 cups peeled, cored, sliced apples
1 teaspoon vanilla or 1 tablespoon dark rum
3/4 cup raisins or blueberries or both
meringue (see Meringue of Pears, page 56)

Melt the butter in a heavy-bottomed saucepan or frying pan. Stir in all the sugar and apples, turning the slices to coat evenly. Cover and cook over low heat for about 20 minutes, or until the apples are tender. Uncover, removed from the heat and mix in the vanilla and raisins. Spoon into a buttered, heatproof glass dish and reserve.

Make the meringue and spread over the top, sprinkle on the nuts, bake and serve according to the instructions for Meringue of Pears. Serves 6-8.

Apple Pan Dowdy

5 large apples

Sauce

1 cup firmly packed brown sugar
1/4 cup all-purpose flour
1 cup boiling water
1/4 cup molasses
1/2 teaspoon salt
1 tablespoon vinegar
1 tablespoon butter
1 teaspoon vanilla
1/2 teaspoon cinnamon
1/2 teaspoon freshly grated nutmeg

Topping Batter

1 cup sifted all-purpose flour
1/2 teaspoon salt
2 teaspoons baking powder
3 tablespoons butter
1/2 cup milk

Pare and quarter the apples and lay them in rows in a well-buttered 8" x 8" cake pan or ovenproof dish.

Combine the brown sugar and 1/4 cup flour in a saucepan. Stir in the water, molasses, salt and vinegar. Simmer until thickened (about 5 minutes). Add the 1 tablespoon butter, vanilla, cinnamon and nutmeg. Remove from the heat and reserve.

Sift together the 1 cup flour, salt and baking powder for the topping batter. Cut in the butter with a pastry blender. Stir in the milk but do not beat.

Pour the sauce over the apples. Spoon the topping batter over the apples and sauce.

Bake at 400 degrees for 35 minutes. Serve warm with a jug of light cream. *Serves 8.*

Steamed Apple Pudding

Judging from the frequency of its appearances in private recipe collections, this was the most popular steamed pudding in the latter half of the nineteenth century. It went by several names — Paradise Pudding, Bachelor's Pudding, Eve's Pudding and, for a touch of class, Duke of Cumberland's Pudding. Basically it was always the same recipe — apples, spices and currants steamed with lots of eggs and butter and served with a caramel sauce.

The idea that steamed puddings are heavy, boring and hard to make is proved wrong by this delicious version.

1/2 cup butter
1/2 cup firmly packed brown sugar
2 eggs, separated
1 teaspoon grated lemon rind
1 cup sifted all-purpose flour
2 teaspoons baking powder
1/2 teaspoon salt
3/4 teaspoon cinnamon
1/2 teaspoon freshly grated nutmeg
1/2 cup currants
1/4 cup brandy
1 3/4 cups grated apples (2 medium apples,
    cored and peeled)

Cream the butter until light and fluffy. Gradually beat in the sugar, the egg yolks, one at a time, and the lemon rind.

Sift together the flour, baking powder, salt and spices. Use 1 tablespoon of these dry ingredients to dredge the currants. Set the currants aside. Add the dry ingredients to the creamed mixture in 3 parts alternating with the brandy in 2 parts. Begin and end with the dry ingredients. Stir in the currants and grated apples. Whip the egg whites until stiff but not dry and fold into the pudding.

Spoon into a well-greased, 1 quart pudding basin that has been dusted lightly with white sugar. Cover with a piece of aluminum foil that has a 1" pleat over the top to let the pudding rise. Tie up securely and place on a rack in a large pot. Pour in boiling water to two-thirds of the way up the pudding basin. Steam 2-2¹/₂ hours. Add more boiling water if necessary to maintain the level. Leave in the dish 5-10 minutes to set. Remove the foil and turn out onto the serving platter.

Serve with Caramel Sauce (see below). *Makes 6 servings.*

Caramel Sauce

1¹/₂ cups firmly packed brown sugar
2 cups boiling water
3 tablespoons cornstarch
¹/₄ teaspoon salt
2 tablespoons cold water
3 tablespoons butter
1 teaspoon vanilla
¹/₂ teaspoon freshly grated nutmeg
2 tablespoons apple brandy, sherry or port

Melt the sugar in a heavy-bottomed saucepan over medium heat. Let it brown slightly and stir in the boiling water. Cook over medium heat until smooth and all the hard particles have dissolved.

Make a paste of cornstarch, salt and cold water. Gradually add to the sauce, stirring to prevent lumps and simmering until the taste of raw cornstarch disappears.

Remove from the heat. Stir in the butter, vanilla, nutmeg and brandy.

Fresh Apple Slices in Green Ginger Syrup

This ingenious modern concoction of green ginger root, fresh apple slices and lemon has none of the sticky sweetness associated with an ice cream sauce. The hotness of the ginger and the crispness of the apple are a great contrast for smooth cold vanilla ice cream. The apple-ginger sauce served at Fenton's restaurant in Toronto was the inspiration for this recipe.

4 ounces green ginger (a root about 6" long)
1 cup warm water
¹/₄ cup white sugar
¹/₄ cup lemon juice
¹/₂ teaspoon grated lemon rind
2 medium-sized sweet apples
1 pint vanilla ice cream

Peel the ginger. Because of all the knobs, this is best done in sections. Grate or chop very finely. There should be about ¹/₃ cup. Place in a bowl, add the water and sugar and stir to dissolve the sugar. Cover and let stand in the refrigerator for 12 hours.

Add the juice and rind. Peel, quarter and core the apples and cut the quarters into very thin slices crosswise. Add to the ginger and syrup, cover and let stand for 12 hours in the refrigerator. Taste and add a little more sugar if desired.

To serve, scoop ice cream into 6 glasses or serving bowls and spoon some of the apples, syrup and ginger over the top. Serve immediately. *Makes 6 servings.*

PICKLES, RELISHES AND PRESERVES

Preserving

There are some important steps to take in preserving. However, once you have gone through the routine two or three times it will become second nature to you.

Wash the jars or sealers, lids, a pair of metal tongs, a metal funnel and a heatproof half cup measure in hot soapy water. Rinse thoroughly and dry either on a rack or with a clean tea towel.

Proceed as follows for preserves sealed with wax. Sterilize the jars. The easiest way to do this is to set the jars on a rack in the oven preheated to 225 degrees and leave them 10-15 minutes. Prepare the wax while the jars are in the oven. Place as many blocks of paraffin wax as will fit into a large, clean tin can (a 1 pound coffee tin is ideal). Bend the rim of the tin to make a spout. Place the tin in a large, shallow saucepan of simmering water and heat until sufficient wax has melted. The can with the wax can be used again as many times as necessary.

Remove the jars from the oven with tongs. Using the sterilized measure and funnel, fill each jar to within 1/2" of the top, taking care not to dribble any jam on the inside of the jar above the jam level. Pour a thin layer of melted wax over the jam, tilting and rotating the jar as the wax is being poured. Let the wax cool completely, then complete the seal with another thin layer of wax. Tilt and rotate the jar as you did before. This ensures a perfect seal right to the edges. Cover the jars and store in a cool, dry and preferably dark place. Once the jar is opened for use, it should be refrigerated.

Sealers and glass and metal screw tops should be sterilized in the same way as the jars. Rubber rings and lids with the rubber ring attached to the lid should never be reused. Dip both the rings and lids briefly in boiling water before using. Be sure to fill sealers right up to the top unless otherwise directed.

Peach and Red Pepper Relish

This is the relish I like to make to give away as presents. The lemon makes it just sour enough, the hot pepper and ginger make it interestingly hot, and the chopped red peppers and peaches give it a beautiful, slightly chunky texture and rich colour.

```
1 lemon
8 cups chopped sweet red peppers (12
        medium peppers)
1/2 cup finely chopped hot red peppers (1
        pepper)
cold water
8 cups chopped peaches
4 cups white sugar
1 1/2 cups white vinegar
2 teaspoons salt
1 tablespoon chopped preserved ginger
1 teaspoon mixed pickling spice
1/4 teaspoon celery seed
```

Pare the yellow zest off the lemon, chop finely and place with the chopped red peppers in a saucepan. Cover with cold water. Bring to the boil uncovered over high heat. Reduce the heat so that the mixture bubbles gently for 8 minutes. Drain, rinse under running cold water and drain thoroughly.

Squeeze the juice out of the lemon. Combine the juice, peppers, peaches, sugar, vinegar, salt and ginger in a preserving kettle. Place the pickling spice and celery seed in a piece of rinsed cheese cloth and add to the ingredients in the kettle. Bring to the boil over high heat, reduce heat to a gentle boil and cook uncovered until thick (about 1-1^1/$_2$ hours). Stir frequently. Remove the spice bag.

Ladle into hot sterilized jars and seal immediately with melted wax. *Yields nine 8-ounce jars.*

Amber Fruit Sauce

This recipe first appeared in Montreal 50 years ago. The peaches, pears, tomatoes and peppers are chopped into equal sized chunks and simmered just long enough to blend the flavours and turn a cinnamony amber colour — hence the name.

> 12 tomatoes
> 12 peaches
> 12 apples
> 12 pears
> 8 onions
> 2 green peppers
> 5 cups white vinegar
> 5 cups white sugar
> 2 tablespoons salt
> ^{1}/$_4$ cup mixed pickling spice

Scald the tomatoes and peaches in boiling water and peel. Core and peel the apples and pears. Peel the onions. Remove the membranes and seeds from the peppers. Chop all these ingredients into pieces about ^{1}/$_2$″ square. There should be 10 cups each of tomatoes, peaches, apples and pears. Put all the chopped ingredients except the peppers into a large preserving kettle.

Add the vinegar, sugar and salt. Tie the pickling spice in a piece of rinsed cheesecloth and add to the other ingredients.

Bring to the boil over high heat, reduce the heat to a gentle boil and cook 30 minutes. Add the

peppers and continue cooking until thickened (about 1-1^1/$_4$ hours). Stir frequently. Remove the spice bag.

Ladle into hot, sterilized jars and seal immediately. Mason or Crown jars are recommended. *Yields 6-7 pints.*

Gingery Apple and Ripe Tomato Chutney

Chutneys are hot, spicy, sweet and sour relishes. Fruit is an essential ingredient, and apples and pears are especially suitable because they create a smooth base for the raisins, preserved ginger, red peppers and spices.

> ^{1}/$_2$ lemon or orange
> 6^1/$_2$ cups chopped, skinned, ripe tomatoes
> 6^1/$_2$ cups chopped, peeled and cored green apples
> ^{1}/$_2$ cup finely chopped sweet red peppers
> 1^1/$_2$ cups chopped onions
> 2^1/$_2$ cups dark seedless raisins
> ^{1}/$_3$ cup chopped preserved ginger
> 3^1/$_2$ cups firmly packed brown sugar
> 1^3/$_4$ cups cider vinegar
> 1 tablespoon salt
> 1 tablespoon mustard seed

Slice the lemon as thinly as possible. Stack the slices in 2 piles, and cut each pile into eighths. Remove any seeds. Combine with all the remaining ingredients in a preserving kettle. Bring to the boil over high heat, reduce heat and cook slowly, stirring frequently, for 2^1/$_2$-3 hours. The chutney will be a rich brown colour, and quite thick.

Pack into hot sterilized jars and seal with melted wax. *Yields ten 8-ounce jars.*

Pear Chutney

This recipe makes a relatively small making of chutney. It's good for the person who wants to try a number of different recipes, or someone who wants a little fine chutney. It's possible, of course, to double or even triple the quantities, but use less salt and a longer cooking period.

2^2/$_3$ cups medium-finely chopped pears
1^2/$_3$ cups chopped ripe tomatoes
1^1/$_4$ cups chopped onions
1 cup chopped sweet red peppers
1^1/$_4$ cups sultana raisins
1 cup firmly packed brown sugar
2 cups cider vinegar
1 tablespoon salt
one 3" stick cinnamon

Combine the ingredients in a heavy-bottomed saucepan. Bring to the boil, reduce the heat and simmer very slowly until the mixture is thick and rich looking. This usually takes about 1^1/$_4$ to 1^1/$_2$ hours. Stir frequently during the cooking period, especially near the end as the chutney could scorch. Remove the cinnamon. Pour into hot sterilized jars and seal with melted wax: *Yields six 6-ounce jars.*

Red Apple and Green Tomato Barbecue Sauce

6 cups finely chopped green tomatoes
4 cups finely chopped, cored, unpeeled red
    apples
1^2/$_3$ cups finely chopped sweet red peppers
2 cups finely chopped onions
1 tablespoon salt
teaspoon freshly ground black pepper
^{1}/$_4$ teaspoon cayenne pepper
2 teaspoon cinnamon
^{3}/$_4$ teaspoon cloves
^{1}/$_4$ teaspoon turmeric

3 cups white sugar
2^1/$_2$ cups white vinegar

Combine all the ingredients in a large preserving kettle. Bring to the boil over high heat, then reduce the heat so that the mixture boils gently. Stirring occasionally, cook until thickened (about 1 hour).

Ladle into hot sterilized jars and seal immediately with melted wax. *Yields about ten 8-ounce jars.*

Spiced Peaches

boiling water
4 quarts small ripe peaches
1 tablespoon whole cloves
8 cups white or firmly packed brown sugar
    (brown sugar and cider vinegar make
    a rich looking brown syrup)
4 cups cider or white vinegar (white sugar
    and white vinegar preserve the rose
    colour of the peaches)
1 cup water
2 cinnamon sticks 3" long, broken into 4
    pieces each

Pour boiling water over the peaches. Leave it only long enough to loosen the skins. Peel the peaches and stick 2 whole cloves in each peach. If your peaches are large, halve and stone them. Stick 1 clove in each half.

Boil the sugar, vinegar, water and cinnamon for 5 minutes in an uncovered preserving kettle.

Add the peaches to the syrup and poach gently until tender (about 15-20 minutes), turning to cook all around.

Remove from heat. Cool and let the peaches stand loosely covered in the syrup overnight.

Pack the peaches into hot sterilized jars. Put a piece of cinnamon in each jar.

Boil up the syrup for 5 minutes. Pour the boiling liquid over the peaches, completely covering them. Seal and store in a cool, dry place. *Yields 8 pints.*

Fresh Apple-Cranberry Relish

   1 medium orange
   1/2 medium lemon
   1 large red-skinned apple
   2 cups cranberries
   1 1/4 cups white sugar
   1/3 cup coarsely chopped almonds or fresh
      walnuts

Wash all the fruit thoroughly. Cut the orange and lemon into quarters, remove any seeds and put through the fine blade of a food grinder.

Quarter and core the apple. Grind the apple and cranberries, using the coarse blade.

Combine the ground fruit with the sugar and nuts. Pack into a container, cover and store in the refrigerator for 2 days before using. Refrigerated, the relish will keep for 2-3 weeks. *Yields about 3 1/2 cups, enough to accompany a 20-pound turkey.*

Mild Spiced Crabapples

This recipe for spiced crabapples does not call for vinegar. Instead, the crabapples are preserved in a mildly spicy sweet syrup with just a hint of lemon. Bright red crabapples are best because they make the preserving syrup a rosy colour. Later the syrup can be used in barbeque sauces or to glaze ham, pork roasts or chops.

   3 quarts crabapples
   4 1/2 cups white sugar
   7 cups water
   1 teaspoon whole cloves
   one 3" cinnamon stick
   2 strips of lemon rind, 1/2" × 3"

Wash the crabapples and remove the blossom ends. Prick each one several times with a fork to prevent bursting.

Combine the sugar and water in a large heavy-bottomed saucepan. Tie the spices and lemon rind in a piece of rinsed cheesecloth and add to the syrup. Bring to the boil, reduce heat and simmer 3-4 minutes. Add the apples, bring back to a very light boil and cook until tender and transparent (about 20 minutes). Handle carefully as you turn them. Remove the spice bag.

Using a slotted spoon pack the crabapples into hot sterilized jars. Boil up the syrup and pour over the fruit. Fill the jars right to the top. Seal and store in a cool dry place. *Yields about 5 pints.*

Jellies

How do you tell when jelly has reached the "jelling point" or has begun to "sheet?" As the juice and sugar boil up together, periodically dip a large metal spoon into the preserving kettle. Hold it horizontally, well above the kettle. At the beginning of the boiling process, the liquid forms 2 streams that flow rapidly off the sides of the spoon. As the jelly approaches the jelling point, the streams slow down, and the last drops come closer to each other, until finally 2 drops meet in the centre of the spoon. They seem to hang onto the spoon, and in doing so, they create a fairly wide piece of jelly. This is "sheeting" or the "jelling point" and occurs at 220 degrees on a candy-making thermometer.

To complete the process, skim the jelly with a metal spoon and pour into hot, sterilized jars. Work quickly because the jelly will soon form a skin over the top that, if poured into the jars, gives the jelly a cloudy appearance.

Apple Jellies

Apple Jelly is as variable as your imagination. It can be used as a glaze for pastries, cakes and puddings, as a garnish for meats, or as an elegant topping for homemade scones. A spoonful melted into meat gravy enriches the flavour.

All apple jelly variations start with a basic Apple Juice (see below). Because the whole apple is used, the colour of the jelly will vary with the variety of apple. My favourites are Red Astrachans, Snows or other red-skinned apples, as they give a lovely blush to the jelly and are particularly suitable for the plain or spicy jelly. Slightly underripe apples are always better for jelly, and if wild apples are available, use them, for they very often produce a flavour unobtainable from standard varieties.

The infusion of herbs gives the jelly quite an unusual and delicious taste.

Apple Jelly

    4 cups Apple Juice (see below)
    3 cups white sugar

Place the juice in a preserving kettle. Bring to the boil over high heat and boil for 3 minutes. Add the sugar and return to the boil. Cook rapidly until the jelly stage is reached (220 degrees on the thermometer). Skim carefully with a cool metal spoon and pour into hot, sterilized jars. Seal immediately with melted wax. *Yields about five 8-ounce jars for each 4 cups of juice.*

Apple Juice for Jelly Making

    6 quarts tart apples, wild if possible
    water (about 12 cups)

Wash the apples and remove the stems and blossom ends. Quarter and slice the apples into a large preserving kettle. Add water until it comes to just below the top of the apples. Bring to the boil, cover, reduce the heat and simmer for 15 minutes or until the apples are mushy. Crush with a mallet or potato masher and cook 5 minutes more. Remove from the heat and pour into a jelly bag. Let drip overnight. Refrigerate any juice you are not using immediately. This juice will keep 2-3 days in the refrigerator before it ferments.

Apple Fresh Herb Jellies

    1 cup leaves and stems of basil, parsley, any
        of the mints or rose geranium
        (loosely packed)
    or
    1/2 cup leaves and stems of thyme, sage,
        summer savory or marjoram
    4 cups Apple Juice (see above)
    3 cups white sugar

Place the herbs in a large, heavy-bottomed saucepan. Bruise with a wooden mallet or potato masher. Add the juice, cover and bring slowly to the boil. Remove from the heat and let stand 20 minutes. Strain out the herbs. Add the sugar and proceed as for Apple Jelly (see page 64).

For the thyme, summer savory or marjoram jelly, a long sprig of the herbs can be suspended upright in the jars with the hot jelly. These jars look terrific. Some recipes suggest putting whole leaves, like sage, basil, mint or geranium into the jars of the hot jelly, but in my experience, the leaves shrivel, float up and stick to the wax. *Yields five 8-ounce jars.*

Elderberry and Apple Jelly

>   3 cups Apple Juice (see page 64)
>   1 cup Elderberry Juice (see below)
>   3 cups white sugar

Place all the juice in a large preserving kettle. Place over high heat, bring to the boil and boil for 5 minutes.

Stir in the sugar, return to the boil and boil rapidly for about 10 minutes, or until the jelly reaches the jelling point (220 degrees on a jelly thermometer).

Skim with a cool metal spoon. Pour quickly into hot, sterilized jars and seal immediately with melted wax. *Yields about four 8-ounce jars.*

Elderberry Juice for Jelly Making

>   5-6 quarts fresh ripe elderberries

Strip the berries off the large stems. Place in a large, heavy-bottomed saucepan (there should be about 8-9 cups of berries). Crush thoroughly with a potato masher and place over low-medium heat. When the juices begin to flow, cover the saucepan and cook gently for 15 minutes.

Place in a jelly bag, and as soon as the bag is cool enough to handle, squeeze out the juice. I recommend that you wear clean rubber gloves for this operation. *Yields about 3 cups of juice.*

Spiced Crabapple Jelly

Red crabapples are so full of pectin and acid that it's hard to keep them from jelling. Spiced Crabapple Jelly is a good recipe for the novice at jelly making. One 6 quart basket makes enough for 2 batches of the following recipe, so by the time all the juice is used up the beginner will be an expert. To make the juice for this jelly, proceed exactly the same as for Apple Juice (see page 64) but simmer for 20-25 minutes before mashing.

>   5¼ cups crabapple juice (see note above and Apple Juice recipe, page 64)
>   ½ cup white vinegar
>   one 4" stick of cinnamon (broken into pieces)
>   1 tablespoon whole cloves or 1 teaspoon whole allspice and 2 teaspoons whole cloves
>   5 cups white sugar

Combine the juice and vinegar in a large preserving kettle. Tie the spices in a piece of rinsed cheesecloth and add to the kettle. Place over high heat, bring to the boil and boil for 3 minutes. Remove the spice bag.

Stir in the sugar, return to the boil and boil hard for 10-15 minutes or until the jelly sheets (220 degrees on the jelly thermometer).

Skim quickly with a cool metal spoon and pour into hot, sterilized jars. Seal immediately with melted wax. *Yields six 8-ounce jars.*

Cranberry and Apple Jelly

Here is another jelly that is good anytime during the fall of the year. Ample supplies of apples and cranberries are available from Thanksgiving to the end of December. Together the fruits produce a lovely, crystal clear red jelly.

    10 large apples
    3 cups cranberries
    6 cups water
    white sugar

Wash the apples, remove the stems and blossom ends and slice roughly into a preserving kettle. Add the cranberries and water. Bring to the boil over high heat, reduce to low and simmer gently for 20 minutes. Crush with a potato masher and cook until all the fruit is tender, about 5 minutes more. Remove from the heat and pour into a jelly bag. Let drip overnight.

Measure the juice into a large preserving kettle. There should be about 4-5 cups. Add an equal quantity of white sugar. Stir thoroughly. Place over high heat and bring to the boil, stirring frequently. Boil rapidly until the jelly sheets (220 degrees on a jelly thermometer).

Remove from the heat and skim off the foamy scum with a clean metal spoon. Immediately pour into hot, sterilized jars and seal with melted wax. *Yields about five 8-ounce jars for every 4 cups of juice.*

Peach and Grape Jam

I prefer to make jams and jellies without adding pectin which tends to make preserves too firm. However there is one real advantage to the pectin method; it greatly reduces cooking time so that more of the fresh flavour of the fruit survives the preserving process. Both peaches and grapes, which are a terrific combination in jam, lack the necessary natural pectin and acid to jell on their own.

    1 quart Concord grapes
    3 cups finely chopped peaches
    1/2 teaspoon grated lemon rind
    2 tablespoons lemon juice
    7 1/2 cups white sugar
    1 bottle liquid pectin

Skin the grapes. Bring the pulp to the boil over medium heat. Reduce heat and simmer covered for 5 minutes. Press through a sieve to remove the seeds. Grind the skins, using a medium blade of a food grinder and combine with the pulp in a preserving kettle. There should be 1 1/2 cups of pulp. Add the peaches, lemon rind, juice and sugar and mix well.

Place over high heat, bring to a full rolling boil and, stirring constantly, boil hard for 1 minute. It is important to be exact about timing when using pectin. Remove from the heat and immediately stir in the pectin. Remove any scum with a metal spoon. Stir and skim 5 minutes. The stirring ensures an even distribution of fruit in the jam.

Ladle into hot sterilized jars and seal immediately with melted wax. *Yields nine 8-ounce jars.*

Honey Pear Butter with Rum

This is an excellent fall preserve to make when the kitchen is cooler and there are still lots of pears. Any juicy ripe pears are good, but they must be juicy because there's no other liquid in the initial cooking. Let any too firm pears ripen out of the basket at room temperature away from sunlight.

As the pears simmer down, they give off an incredibly intense pear aroma and gradually turn into a thick buckwheat honey-coloured butter.

    4 pounds ripe juicy pears (8-10 pears)
    1/4 cup orange juice
    1/2 teaspoon grated orange rind
    2 cups white sugar

1/2 cup clover honey
1/4 teaspoon freshly grated nutmeg
2 tablespoons rum

Wash the pears, remove the stems and cut out blossom ends. Chop coarsely but evenly and place in a heavy-bottomed saucepan over low heat. Cover and cook for 30 minutes or until tender and pulpy. Stir frequently to prevent the pears from sticking. Press through a sieve or food mill with a fine disc. There should be about 5 cups of sauce.

Put the sauce, juice, rind, sugar and honey into a clean, heavy-bottomed saucepan. Cook over low heat so that the sauce bubbles very gently. Stir very frequently, especially as the sauce thickens. It will take about 2 1/2 hours for the sauce to reduce by half into a thick butter. To test for doneness, place a spoonful on a saucer and turn over. If the pear butter is done, it will not fall off. Be sure to do this test over the sink.

Taste, add the nutmeg if desired and stir in the rum. Ladle into hot sterilized jars and seal with melted wax. *Yields eight to nine 4-ounce jars.*

West Coast Apple Ginger Sauce

An amazing number of turn-of-the-century West Coast recipes combine apples, lemons and ginger. Unlike apple butter where a smooth consistency is the goal, the apples in Apple Ginger are meant to be in separate slices with a tangy, gingery sauce. This makes an unusual sauce for vanilla ice cream.

3 lemons
6 ounces green ginger (two 4" pieces)
3 cups water
6 cups white sugar
3 pounds small apples

Pare the yellow zest off the lemons. Peel and chop the ginger into medium-fine pieces. There should be about 3/4 cup of chopped ginger. Combine the zest, ginger and water in a saucepan. Cover and bring to the boil, then remove from the heat and leave 12-24 hours to steep.

Strain the liquid into a large, heavy-bottomed saucepan. Discard the lemon zest and all but 1/4 cup of the ginger. Chop this finely and return to the liquid. Stir in the sugar. Bring to the boil and boil 5 minutes.

Meanwhile peel, quarter and core the apples and divide them into eighths. To keep the apple from turning brown while you work, drop slices into a large bowl of water. Drain the apples and add to the ginger syrup. Bring back to a gentle simmer and cook until the apples are tender and translucent, about 30 minutes. Squeeze the lemons and strain the juice into the apple-ginger mixture. Stir gently.

Fill hot, sterilized pint jars right up to the top and seal. Alternately, pour into a large, hot, sterilized glass container, cool and store covered in the refrigerator. For the latter method of storage, plan on using within 3-4 weeks.

Classic Peach Marmalade

Peach marmalade has been a classic Canadian favorite for generations. Sometimes it's called jam and sometimes conserve. But whatever the name, its constant features are oranges, peaches and cherries.

> 3 oranges
> 1 cup water
> 9 cups white sugar
> 8 cups peeled, finely chopped peaches
> one 6-ounce bottle maraschino cherries
> 1 cup slivered, blanched almonds

Put the oranges through the medium blade of a grinder, or slice very finely and cut the slices in eighths. Remove seeds before grinding or after slicing. Place in a small saucepan with the water, cover and simmer over low heat until the peel is tender, about 20-30 minutes.

Place the peel mixture, sugar and peaches in a large preserving kettle. Drain the cherry juice into the kettle. Cut the cherries into quarters and reserve. Stir the mixture thoroughly.

Place over high heat, bring to the boil, reduce the heat and cook uncovered, at a good simmer, until the marmalade thickens, and the peaches are translucent. This takes about 1 hour. Stir very frequently, especially near the end of the cooking time. Add the cherries and almonds and cook for 5 minutes.

Ladle into hot, sterilized jars and seal with melted wax. *Yields twelve 8-ounce jars.*

Brandied Peach Marmalade

Proceed as for the Classic Peach Marmalade, stirring in ¼ cup brandy just before filling the jars. *Yields twelve 8-ounce jars.*

Pear and Raisin Conserve

Out of any hundred pear conserve recipes ninety-eight are for pear and ginger. However in *this* one, pears are simmered with golden sultanas, oranges and lemons and come out a beautiful amber colour. The walnut halves are added at the end of the cooking to give it crunch. It's recipes like this that make home preserving worthwhile.

> 2 oranges
> ½ lemon
> 1 cup cold water
> 11 cups chopped, peeled and cored pears
> 1½ cups bleached sultana raisins
> 8 cups white sugar
> 1 cup fresh walnuts, roughly chopped

Squeeze the juice from the oranges and lemon. Strain into a preserving kettle. Grind the orange and lemon peel, using the fine blade of a food grinder. Mix the peel with water in a saucepan, bring to the boil over high heat, reduce heat and simmer uncovered 20 minutes. Drain thoroughly and add peel to the juice. Stir the pears, raisins and sugar into the rind and juice.

Bring to the boil over high heat, then reduce heat so that the conserve boils gently for 1 hour. By this time the fruit will be tender and the juices reduced. Add the walnuts and simmer another 15 minutes. Stir frequently throughout the cooking period.

Ladle into hot, sterilized jars and seal immediately with melted wax. *Yields about eleven 8-ounce jars.*

Peach and Raisin Conserve

Proceed according to instructions for Pear and Raisin Conserve, substituting finely chopped peaches for the pears and slivered, blanched almonds for the walnuts.

Brandied Peaches

It isn't hard to convince people that making preserves is economical, useful and enjoyable and that the results are better than anything on the market. But elegant? I submit Brandied Peaches for the final test. Their appearance and taste are impressive, perfect for an unexpected dinner party. Serve over good vanilla ice cream, or in a glass topped with unsweetened whipped cream or sour cream or use as a filling for flamed crepes, tarts or cakes. For added zest, I recommend strips of orange peel or whole cloves.

>3^1/$_2$ cups white sugar
>1 cup water
>4 pounds peaches (16 small peaches)
>8 whole cloves or 4 strips of orange peel,
> ^{1}/$_2$" $\times$ 3" (optional)
>1 cup brandy

Combine the sugar and water in a large preserving kettle. Bring to the boil and boil vigorously for 3 minutes.

Peel the peaches and place them whole in the preserving kettle with the syrup and optional cloves or peel. Bring back to the boil, then reduce the heat so that the peaches are simmering in the liquid. Continue cooking until the fruit is tender, about 15-20 minutes.

Remove the peaches with a slotted spoon, and divide equally among 4 hot, sterilized pint jars. Place 2 cloves or 1 strip of peel in each jar if desired.

Increase the heat under the syrup and boil vigorously for 4 minutes. Remove from the heat and add the brandy. Fill the jars with the hot syrup and seal. *Yields 4 pints.*

Processing Applesauce, Peaches and Pears

Use pint or quart Mason jars. Check the top to see that there are no nicks or cracks in the glass. Wash in hot, soapy water, rinse and sterilize in the oven for 15 minutes at 225 degrees. Always buy new lids but use the old screw rings unless they are rusty or dented. The lids and rings do not need to be sterilized. But they must be dipped in boiling water before being put on the jars, so have a saucepan of water simmering on the back of the stove while the jars are being sterilized and the fruit cooks. In addition, have ready enough boiling water to fill the processor with the jars in it.

Fill the sterilized jars with the hot applesauce, peaches or pears and syrup, leaving ^{1}/$_2$" headspace at the top. Run a knife along the inside of the jar to let out air bubbles. Wipe the rims of the jars with a clean cloth. Put on the lid and screw on the ring as tightly as possible. Place the jars on the rack in the empty processor. Make sure that there is at least a 1" space between the jars.

Pour boiling water into the processor, but not directly onto the jars. Fill the processor so that the water level is 2" above the jars. Cover, place over maximum heat and bring to a full rolling boil. Time from this moment. All of these fruits need 15 minutes of vigorous boiling. Mincemeat can also be processed this way, but allow 25 minutes processing.

When the processing time is over, remove the processor from the heat, uncover and lift out the jars with a jar lifter. Place 1" apart right side up on a thick, dry towel out of drafts. Let cool for 12 hours.

Check the seal before storing the fruit in a cool, dry place. If the seal is good, the lid will have been sucked into a concave shape, and if tapped with a spoon, a clear ringing sound is heard. If any jars do not have a good seal, store in the refrigerator and use within 3-4 days.

Preserved Applesauce

Why preserved applesauce when apples are available virtually year round? It's because the taste of the August and early September apples is unique, and they make a beautifully-textured sauce. What's more, they are often small and therefore usually cheaper than later apples for which storage charges also must be added. Since they are at their peak for such a short time, they need to be used up quickly. The best varieties for this recipe are Red Astrachan, Melba, Transparent, Lodi and Duchess. Each one has a special flavour and colour.

Of course, applesauce freezes well, too. Instead of processing the sauce in jars, fill plastic containers, leaving 1/2" headspace and freeze.

Applesauce is a handy ingredient for cakes, puddings, pies, cookies and stuffings. Naturally it's delicious on its own for desserts or for breakfasts.

> 3 pounds apples (15 small apples)
> 1 cup water
> 1/2-3/4 cup white sugar or honey or a
>   combination

Remove the stems and blossom ends from the apples. Wash and slice into a large saucepan. Add the water, cover and bring to the boil over high heat. Reduce heat immediately and simmer until the apples are all tender and broken up. Crush with a potato masher to help the process. Total cooking time will be about 15-20 minutes.

Pass the apples through a sieve, ricer or food mill, using the fine disk. Return the applesauce to a clean saucepan and add sweetening to taste. (Applesauce can be preserved without sugar if desired.) Heat through, stirring to prevent scorching the bottom.

Process according to the directions on page 69 and store in a cool, dark, dry place. Double or triple quantities as desired. *Yields 2 pints.*

Preserved Pears

> 4 1/2 cups water
> 1 2/3 cups white sugar
> 1 strip of orange rind, 1/2" × 3"
> 4 quarts medium pears (6-7 pounds or 18-20
>   pears)
> 5-6 whole cloves or 5-6 1/4"-cubes of
>   preserved ginger or a 1" stick of
>   cinnamon broken into 5-6 pieces (all
>   of these are optional)

Combine the water, sugar and orange rind in a large preserving kettle. Bring to the boil, stirring to dissolve the sugar. Reduce the heat to simmer while preparing the pears.

Peel, halve and core the pears. Add to the syrup and bring back to the boil over high heat. Reduce the heat and simmer 3 minutes in all. Remove the rind.

Divide the pears and syrup evenly among 5-6 hot sterilized pint jars, leaving 1/2" space at the top. Add a clove, a piece of ginger or cinnamon to each jar if desired.

Proceed with the processing according to the instructions on page 69. Store in a cool, dark, dry place. *Yields 5-6 pints.*

Home Canned Peaches

Preserving peaches, is a long-established harvest tradition. Every August, Canadian women "put down" bushels, not just baskets, of peaches. In Ontario and British Columbia many people picked their own peaches so they could afford more. Only the advent of the freezer put an end to this. Canned peaches, as they were called even though most people preserved them in quart sealers, were a very common winter dessert. While no one would claim that they are the same as fresh peaches, they still taste good, and the effort required to preserve them has its reward in January when you open a jar.

2 cups white sugar
3 cups water
3 quarts medium peaches

Combine the sugar and water in a large preserving kettle. Heat to the boiling point, stirring to dissolve the sugar. Reduce the heat, but keep the liquid hot until the peaches are ready.

Peel the peaches, cut them in half and remove the stones. Add the peach halves to the syrup, bring rapidly back to the boil and cook for 3 minutes.

Divide the peaches and syrup evenly among 5-6 hot, sterilized pint jars, leaving 1/2" space at the top. Process according to the instructions on page 69.

Store in a cool, dry, dark place. *Yields 5-6 pints*.

Frozen Peaches

Peaches are one of the easiest and best fruits to freeze. But it's vital to choose ripe, juicy peaches free from blemishes. I have found that peaches which are ripe in August are better than the later varieties.

The following recipe serves 4-6 people. You can double or triple as desired, but be sure to pack the peaches into bags or freezer containers of the size you plan to eat in one sitting. Thawed peaches have a tendency to turn brown and should be eaten immediately.

The quantity of ascorbic acid needed to keep the peaches from browning varies with the brand of acid used. Read the instructions for the acid carefully and adjust the amount if necessary. It is possible to reduce the quantity of sugar to 1/2 cup per 4 cups of fruit.

1/2-2/3 cup white sugar
1/2-1 teaspoon ascorbic acid
4 cups sliced peaches

Combine the sugar and ascorbic acid. Sprinkle over the peaches. Stir to distribute evenly through the peaches. Pack into freezer bags or plastic containers.

Thaw covered and serve as soon as the fruit is free of ice crystals.

Frozen peaches, thawed to the stage where you can break up the package into chunks with your hands, make an easy peach sherbet. Whip in the blender and serve immediately in chilled glasses topped with a dab of whipped cream or use as a sauce over vanilla ice cream.

Drying Apples

The Mennonites in Ontario's Waterloo County still get together in groups to "schnitz" apples. Even though the word actually comes from the German verb meaning "to cut," it has become synonymous with making dried apples. In the nineteenth century, farmers of all ethnic backgrounds had apple paring and slicing "bees." These bees provided an opportunity for men and women to get together, have a good chat and even do a bit of romancing.

Drying apples is not a mysterious process. In fact it's relatively easy and requires no special equipment.

Peel, core and slice the apples into thickish slices, as for a pie. Spread the slices in a single layer on racks or screens and place in a warm spot where there's good air circulation and no flies. Turn them once or twice until they are dry. Traditionally, these racks were suspended from the kitchen ceiling, near the stove.

If you don't have a supply of racks, thread a large darning needle with a yard or so of light string. Thread the prepared apple slices loosely onto the string as if they were beads. Loop the strings up somewhere out of the way in the kitchen. The strings should not touch each other as the apples tend to stick to each other slightly as they dry. After a day, move the slices around on the string, separating them so the slices don't stick to each other. Repeat this separating once more after 2-3 days. After a week or so, the apples will be dry enough to pack away. I usually store mine in a covered crock, but they can also be stored in loosely-tied paper bags in a dry, dark cupboard.

Rich Mincemeat

1 pound finely minced lean round steak
water
3 cups cider
4 cups firmly packed brown sugar
1 cup finely chopped or shredded suet
6 cups peeled, cored, grated apples
1 pound seeded raisins
1 pound sultanas
1 pound currants
2/3 cup citron peel
1/3 cup orange peel
1/3 cup lemon peel
3/4 cup blanched slivered almonds
1 1/2 teaspoons salt
2 teaspoons allspice
1 teaspoon cinnamon
1 teaspoon cloves
1 1/2 teaspoons ginger
1 teaspoon mace
2 teaspoons nutmeg
1 teaspoon grated lemon rind
2 tablespoons lemon juice
1 teaspoon grated orange rind
1/4 cup orange juice
1 1/2 cups brandy or rum

Place the beef in a saucepan, add enough water to cover, stir and place over high heat. Bring to the boil, reduce heat and simmer 5-6 minutes. Drain off the liquid and either chop the meat with a knife or whirl in the blender to soften the fibres thoroughly.

Meanwhile, pour the cider into a large preserving kettle and boil vigorously over high heat until reduced to about 1 1/2 cups. Add the brown sugar and return to the boil. Stir in the meat and all the remaining ingredients, except the brandy. Bring back to the boil over medium heat, stirring frequently to prevent sticking. Reduce the heat so the mincemeat simmers gently for 1 hour. By this time, the apples should be transparent, the fruit plumped and the all-over consistency thick.

Remove from the heat, stir in 3/4 cup of the brandy and pack into a clean crock. Cool. Pour remaining brandy over the top, cover the top with plastic wrap and tie a string or elastic firmly around the top. Store in the refrigerator. Allow 2 weeks to mellow before using.

The mincemeat can also be packed in hot,

sterilized jars and stored in a cool place for up to 8 weeks. If you are doing this, either add all of the brandy to the mincemeat or pack the jars leaving 1/2" on top, then fill the jars with brandy and seal. To keep longer than 8 weeks, stir all the brandy into the mincemeat and process according to the instructions on page 69.

Use about 3 cups per pie, depending on the size of the pie plate. *Yields 12-13 cups.*

Pear Mincemeat

    1 orange
    1 lemon
    15 cups finely chopped or grated, peeled and
        cored pears
    1/4 cup orange marmalade
    1/2 cup citron peel
    1/2 cup chopped candied pineapple
    1 1/2 pounds golden sultana raisins
    1 pound seedless raisins
    4 cups white sugar

    1 1/2 cups cider, white wine, apple juice or
        apple wine (or a combination)
    1 1/2 teaspoons allspice
    2 teaspoons cinnamon
    2 teaspoons ginger
    2 teaspoons nutmeg
    1 teaspoon cloves
    1/2 cup butter
    1/2 cup light rum

Put the orange and lemon through the fine blade of a food grinder. Combine with the rest of the ingredients, except the rum, in a large preserving kettle. Bring to the boil, then reduce the heat and simmer for 45 minutes, or until the mincemeat is thick and a rich caramel brown. Stir occasionally. Add the rum.

Pack in sterilized jars, seal and store in a cool place. The mincemeat will keep 2-3 months. If you want to keep it longer, process in boiling water according to the instructions on page 69.

Yields approximately 16 cups or enough for 4-6 pies, depending on the size of the pie plate.

MEAT AND FISH MAIN COURSES

Roast Turkey with Applesauce Sausage Dressing

one 20-22 pound turkey (allow 1/2-3/4 pound per person)

Dressing.

2 pounds sausage meat
3 cups chopped onions
3 cups chopped celery
1/2 teaspoon salt
1/2 teaspoon freshly ground pepper
4-5 teaspoons dried crushed sage
1 teaspoon dried crushed thyme, marjoram or summer savory
18 slices wholewheat bread
1/2 cup currants or raisins (optional)
1/2 cup coarsely chopped fresh walnuts or unblanched almonds (optional)
1 cup Thick Unsweetened Applesauce (see page 41)
1/4 cup soft butter
1 teaspoon dry mustard

Gravy

turkey neck and giblets
1 small onion
1 small carrot
a few celery leaves
1 bay leaf
2 stalks of parsley
cold water
3-4 tablespoons Kneaded Butter (see page 80)
2 tablespoons Apple Jelly (see page 64)
salt and pepper

Wipe out the cavities of the turkey with a damp cloth. Dry the outside and set to one side.

Sauté the sausage meat over medium heat in a large frying pan until it is no longer pink. Add the onion, celery, salt, pepper and herbs. Reduce the heat to low and cook for 15 minutes.

Cube the bread, being sure to include the crusts. Place in a large mixing bowl and add the currants and nuts. Pour the sausage mixture over the bread. Mix in the cup of applesauce or as much as is required to make a moist but not soggy dressing. Taste and add more salt, pepper and sage as desired (the quantity of sage in a dressing is really a personal decision).

Stuff the turkey, body cavity first, then the neck cavity. Skewer or sew up the openings. Truss the turkey. Make sure the turkey skin is dry. Set breast side up on a rack in an open roasting pan. Mix together the soft butter and mustard. Smear all over the turkey. Place a piece of cheesecloth over the breast.

Roast at 325 degrees, basting frequently, for 7 1/2-8 1/2 hours. The temperature on a meat thermometer inserted in the thigh should register 190 degrees. Remove the cheesecloth. Place the turkey on a heated platter, sprinkle with salt, cover loosely and let stand in a warm place for 15-20 minutes.

As soon as the turkey is in the oven, place the neck, giblets, onion, carrot, celery leaves, bay leaf and parsley in a saucepan. Cover with cold water. Bring to the boil, reduce the heat and simmer gently for 2 hours or until tender. Strain the broth, place in the refrigerator and reserve for the gravy. Chop the giblets and meat from the neck and refrigerate.

When the turkey is cooked, drain the fat from the drippings. Blend the kneaded butter into the drippings. Place over medium heat and cook until thickened. Add as much of the giblet stock as is necessary to make a smooth thickened gravy. Stir in the jelly and reserved giblets. Heat until the jelly has melted and the gravy is steaming. Add salt and pepper to taste and pour into a heated gravy boat to serve.

Garnish the turkey with parsley or celery leaves and put paper frills on the drumsticks.

Sauerkraut Dressed Duck

The sauerkraut that you make at home or buy at the market or delicatessen has a crisper texture and none of the harsh, sour taste associated with canned sauerkraut. It's always a good idea to rinse the excess salt off before beginning to cook sauerkraut and to wait until the duck is cooked before adding more salt.

> 1/4 cup butter
> 1 cup chopped onions
> 1/4 cup chopped celery
> 1 cup rye bread cubes
> 1/4 teaspoon freshly ground pepper
> 3/4 teaspoon caraway seeds
> 1 tablespoon finely chopped parsley
> 1/4 teaspoon dried, crushed sage
> 1 tablespoon brown sugar
> 1/4 cup raisins (optional)
> 3 cups sauerkraut, loosely packed
> 2 cups chopped, cored, unpeeled red apples
> 1/4 cup cider or white wine
> one 6-pound duck
> 1 teaspoon dried mustard
> 1/4 teaspoon freshly ground pepper
> 1/2 cup cider
> salt
> 1-2 teaspoons Kneaded Butter (see page 80)
> 1/2 cup stock
> parsley

Melt the butter over medium-low heat. Add the onions and celery and sauté until the vegetables are limp. Remove the vegetables and reserve. Add the bread cubes and sauté 4-5 minutes until lightly browned. Return the vegetables to the frying pan and add the pepper, caraway seeds, parsley, sage, brown sugar and raisins. Stir together and remove from the heat. Turn into a large mixing bowl.

Rinse the sauerkraut under cold running water and drain thoroughly. Combine with the apple and the 1/4 cup cider in a saucepan. Cover and cook 10 minutes over medium-low heat until the sauerkraut is limp. Stir as the sauerkraut and apples are cooking. Drain, adding any juice to the 1/2 cup apple cider. Mix the drained sauerkraut and apples with the sautéed vegetables. Cool.

Remove excess fat from the cavity of the duck. Trim the neck skin. Stuff the duck, cavity first, then the neck. Skewer or sew the openings. Truss the duck and prick evenly in about a dozen places. Rub the duck all over with the mustard and the last 1/4 teaspoon pepper. Place breast down on a rack in an open roasting pan.

Roast 45 minutes at 350 degrees. Drain off the fat. Turn breast side up and roast 1 1/4-1 1/2 hours. Baste periodically with the 1/2 cup apple cider until it is all used up. Do not baste with the pan juices. The duck is cooked when a meat thermometer registers 165 degrees, or when the thigh feels soft when pressed. The duck skin should be a magnificent brown and crusty.

Remove from the oven, sprinkle with salt and place on a warm platter. Cover lightly and keep in a warm place to rest for 10-15 minutes.

Skim off all the fat from the pan juices. Mix in the kneaded butter, place over medium heat and cook until thickened. Add salt to taste. If more gravy is desired, add up to 1/2 cup hot stock, cooking water drained off mild vegetables or plain water. Adjust the thickening. Pour into a warm gravy boat and serve with the duck.

Garnish the platter with lots of parsley and serve immediately. When carving, be sure to include a fair portion of the crunchy skin with each serving. *A 6-pound duck is enough for 4 people.*

Cider and Apple Chicken

one 2¹/₂-3 pound frying chicken or 6 breasts
    or legs and thighs
¹/₄ cup flour
1 teaspoon salt
¹/₂ teaspoon freshly ground pepper
¹/₄ teaspoon dried, crushed thyme
3 tablespoons butter
3 tablespoons oil
¹/₂ cup finely chopped onions
1¹/₂ cups sliced mushrooms
1 cup sliced, peeled and cored apples
³/₄ cup cider, fresh or fermented
1 tablespoon lemon juice
2 teaspoons sugar
salt and freshly ground pepper
2 tablespoons finely chopped parsley
¹/₄ teaspoon grated lemon rind

Cut the chicken into serving pieces, removing the back bone, neck and wing tips up to first joint to use for stock or soup. Pat the chicken parts dry with paper towelling. Do not wash the chicken.

Combine the flour, salt, pepper and thyme in a paper bag. Shake the chicken a few pieces at a time in this mixture.

Heat the butter and oil in a large frying pan until they foam. Add the chicken in one layer and sauté until golden brown on all sides. Regulate the heat so that the butter does not burn.

Scatter the onions, mushrooms and apples over the chicken, letting some fall between the pieces. Pour the cider and lemon juice over the top and sprinkle with the sugar. Cover, bring to the boil, then reduce the heat to low and cook 20-30 minutes, or until the chicken is cooked through. Turn once. It is easy to tell when the chicken is cooked, pierce the thickest piece with a skewer, and if the juices run clear the chicken is cooked.

Remove the chicken and place on a heated platter. Stir the pan juices, onions, mushrooms and apples, removing any crusty bits from the frying-pan. Taste and add more salt, pepper and sugar if desired.

Pour the sauce over the chicken. Combine the parsley and grated lemon rind and sprinkle over the top. *Enough for 4-6 servings.*

Roast Butt of Pork with Prune and Apple Stuffing

Prunes and apples are an excellent combination for pork, and I recommend this stuffing for a boneless butt roast. This cut is one of the easiest to debone, and when you remove the bone, there is a little pocket along the middle and one side. Simply extend the pocket with a sharp knife to accommodate the stuffing and sew it up neatly with heavy thread and a darning needle. The bone can be used for soup or roasted in the pan, so that it adds its flavour to the drippings.

This recipe needn't be restricted to a pork butt, as this quantity will stuff a large boneless pork shoulder, 6-8 thick pork chops slit horizontally, 3-4 tenderloins or a length of spare ribs, folded in half and skewered up. Use it also to stuff a 5-6 pound roasting chicken or duck. Increase the recipe by half for a 10 pound goose and double for a 12-14 pound turkey.

Serve the roast with buttered Brussels sprouts, lemony green beans or braised celery and a dry red wine.

one 4-5 pound boneless butt or one 4¹/₂-5¹/₂
    pound butt with the bone in

Marinade

¹/₄ cup fresh or fermented cider
2 tablespoons oil
1 tablespoon lemon juice
¹/₄ teaspoon freshly ground pepper
1 bay leaf
¹/₈ teaspoon ginger
¹/₄ teaspoon dried crushed basil or sage
2 stalks parsley
1 small carrot, scraped and sliced
1 small onion, peeled and sliced

Dressing

> $1/3$ cup butter
> $1/4$ cup finely chopped onions
> 1 cup unpeeled, cored, chopped apples
> $1/2$ teaspoon dried crushed basil
> $1/2$ teaspoon dried crushed sage
> $1/2$ teaspoon freshly ground pepper
> $3/4$ teaspoon salt
> $1/4$ teaspoon grated lemon rind
> 1 teaspoon lemon juice
> $1/2$ cup chopped fresh walnuts
> 2 cups stale but not dry breadcrumbs from homemade-style white or brown bread
> $2/3$ cup halved, pitted, uncooked prunes
> $1/4$ cup fresh cider, apple juice or orange juice

Coating

> 2 tablespoons melted butter
> $1/2$ teaspoon dry mustard
> freshly ground pepper
> pinch of ginger

Gravy

> 2 tablespoons Kneaded Butter (see page 80)
> salt, freshly ground pepper
> 2 cups stock, vegetable cooking liquid or water

Wipe the roast with a damp cloth and trim off any excess fat or skin. If the butt is not deboned, remove the bone. Extend the opening to form a pocket 6"-7" long and 4"-5" deep in the meat. Place the meat in a glass bowl.

Combine the marinade ingredients and pour over the meat, rubbing the liquid into all the crevices. Cover and refrigerate 12-24 hours. Turn 3-4 times. When ready to proceed with the stuffing, remove the meat from the marinade and wipe dry inside and out with paper towelling. Strain the marinade, reserving the liquid for the gravy and discarding the rest.

To prepare the dressing, melt the butter in a medium frying pan and add the onion and apple. Sauté over low-medium heat until translucent. Add the herbs, salt, pepper, lemon rind, juice and nuts. Cook gently for 5 minutes or so for the flavours to blend.

Place the breadcrumbs, prunes and juice in a large mixing bowl. Pour the sautéed ingredients over them and blend together. Cool slightly so that the dressing can be handled.

Stuff the dressing into the pocket of the roast. Extend the pocket again if necessary. Sew up the opening with heavy thread or light string and wipe dry. Stir together the ingredients for the coating and brush over the meat. Roast on a rack in an uncovered roasting pan at 350 degrees for 30 minutes per pound.

Remove from the pan and sprinkle with salt. Set on a heated platter, cover lightly and let stand 10-15 minutes in a warm place.

Skim the fat off the pan drippings. Stir in the marinade liquid and blend in the kneaded butter. Place over medium heat. Whisk in the stock and cook until thickened and smooth. Work up all the nice brown crusty parts from the roaster. Add salt and freshly ground pepper to taste. Strain the gravy and pour into a warmed gravy boat.

Garnish the platter with spiced fruit or a lot of parsley. *Serves 6-7.*

Cider Sauced Butterfly Pork Chops

This is a good dish for a friendly dinner party. Serve the chops with buttered new potatoes tossed in chopped parsley and chives or caraway seeds. Crisp green beans and braised celery are excellent, too.

2 tablespoons butter
2 tablespoons oil
4 butterfly pork chops
2 medium onions, chopped
1 clove garlic, crushed
$1/2$ teaspoon salt
$1/4$ teaspoon freshly ground pepper
1 tablespoon lemon juice
$3/4$ cup fresh or fermented cider
parsley

Melt the butter in a large frying pan and add the oil. Heat until bubbling but not burning. Dry the pork chops well in paper towelling and brown on both sides in the fat. Be careful not to let the butter and oil burn. Remove the chops and reserve.

Add the onions and garlic to the frying pan. Sauté over medium-low heat until translucent. Push to one side, return the chops to the pan and then spoon the onion and garlic over the chops. Sprinkle on the salt, pepper and lemon juice. Pour the cider around the chops. Cover and bring to the boil. Reduce the heat immediately and simmer 20 minutes or so or until tender.

Place the chops on a heated serving platter. Boil the cider sauce over high heat until thickened but not syrupy. Spoon some of the sauce over each chop. Garnish with parsley and serve. *Serves 4.*

Cinnamon Pork Chops

12 thin pork chops, $1/4$" thick
3 tablespoons flour
$1/2$ teaspoon salt
$1/2$ teaspoon freshly ground pepper

$1/4$ teaspoon crushed dried thyme
2 tablespoons oil
2 tablespoons butter
$1/3$ cup water or cider
3 large apples
2 medium onions
$1/3$ cup firmly packed brown sugar
1 tablespoon cinnamon
2 tablespoon lemon juice

Dry the pork chops on paper towelling. Combine the flour, salt, pepper and thyme in a paper bag. Shake the pork chops in the mixture, a few at a time, to coat them lightly.

Melt the oil and butter in a frying pan. Sauté the pork chops a few at a time, until golden brown on both sides. Regulate the heat so that the fat does not burn. Add more oil and butter if necessary. Remove the chops and reserve. Add the water to the frying pan. Stir and cook over medium heat until all the brown bits have come off the pan. Remove from the heat and reserve.

Core but do not peel the apples. Peel the onions. Slice the apples and onions thinly.

Combine the brown sugar and cinnamon.

In a wide, heatproof casserole place a layer of half the apples and onions, half the sugar and cinnamon and all of the chops, overlapping them to fit. Then add a second layer of the rest of the apples and onions and the sugar mixture. Sprinkle on the lemon juice and pan liquids.

Cover tightly and bake at 325 degrees for $1 1/2$ hours.

Serve 2 chops and a spoonful of the juicy apple mixture with each portion. *Serves 6.*

Pork and Apple Pie

$1 1/2$ pounds lean, boneless pork (from the butt or shoulder)
$3/4$ cup finely chopped onions
$1 1/2$ teaspoons dried crushed sage
3 tablespoons finely chopped parsley
$1/4$ teaspoon dried crushed thyme

1 teaspoon salt
1/4 teaspoon freshly ground pepper
2 tablespoons flour
1/4 cup finely grated dry bread crumbs
2 tablespoons lemon juice
2 cups peeled, cored, sliced tart apples
2 tablespoons stock or water
4 cups hot mashed potatoes
1/3 cup hot milk
2 tablespoons melted butter

Cut the pork into 1/2" cubes. Place in a bowl with the onions. Combine the herbs, salt, pepper, flour and bread crumbs and toss with the pork and onions to coat all the pieces evenly.

In a separate bowl, sprinkle the lemon juice over the apples.

Place about one-third of the pork mixture into the bottom of a greased 8-cup ovenproof dish. Add half the apples, another third of the pork, the rest of the apples and the remaining pork. Sprinkle on the stock.

Cover the dish tightly with aluminum foil and tie with string. Bake at 325 degrees for 2 hours. The meat should be tender. Remove the cover.

Mix the hot milk into the mashed potatoes and pipe or spread over the pork and apples. Brush with the melted butter. Broil 4" from the heat for 3-5 minutes or until the top is browned. Let stand 5 minutes before serving. *Serves 6.*

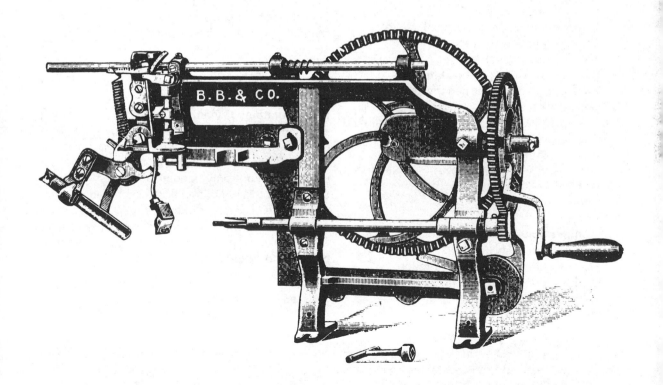

Apple and Tarragon Stuffed Whitefish

Apples and fish are a terrific and very underappreciated combination in Canada. Perhaps the following recipe will help improve the situation.

If when cooking a smaller fish there is extra stuffing, bake it uncovered in an ovenproof dish at the same time as the fish. When the fish is cooked, place it on a warmed oval platter, remove the thread or skewers and spoon the extra stuffing along the opening. Garnish the platter with lemon slices and parsley, watercress or celery leaves.

Dressing

> 1/4 cup butter
> 3/4 cup finely chopped onions
> 1 cup chopped celery
> 2 cups peeled, cored, chopped apples
> 1/4 teaspoon grated lemon rind
> 1/4 cup chopped parsley
> 3/4 teaspoon dried crushed tarragon
> 1/4 teaspoon dried crushed thyme
> 1/2 teaspoon salt
> 1/2 cup cooked rice, preferably brown or wild
> 1 tablespoon lemon juice
> one 3-4 pound fish such as whitefish,
>   pickerel or lake trout (2 smaller fish
>   work well, too)

Coating

> 2 tablespoons soft butter
> 1/4 teaspoon freshly ground pepper
> 1/4 teaspoon dried crushed tarragon
> 2 tablespoons lemon juice
> salt
> one lemon, sliced
> celery leaves or parsley

Melt the 1/4 cup butter in a frying pan over medium-low heat. Add the vegetables and apples and sauté gently until limp (about 5 minutes). Add the rind, herbs and 1/2 teaspoon salt and continue cooking 10 minutes to blend the flavours. Remove from the heat and stir in the rice and lemon juice. Cool until easy to handle.

Wipe the interior cavity and exterior of the fish with a damp cloth. Fill with the stuffing and sew closed with a darning needle and heavy thread.

Wipe the outside of the fish as dry as possible. Smear half of the soft butter on one side and lay buttered side down in an oval ovenproof dish. Smear the top side with the remaining butter and sprinkle on the tarragon and pepper. Pour the remaining 2 tablespoons of lemon juice on the fish.

Bake at 375 degrees, allowing 10 minutes for each pound plus 10 minutes. Baste near the end of the baking time with the accumulated pan juices.

Remove from the pan, salt, place on a warmed platter and remove the thread. Pour the pan juices over the fish or serve in a small pitcher. Garnish the platter with the sliced lemon and celery leaves. *Serves 4-5.*

Kneaded Butter

For generations Canadians have been thickening gravy and sauces with flour shaken up in a jar with cold water. It's time to stop. Kneaded butter or *Beurre manié*, as it is known in France where it originates, is not only handier but easier. Make up a supply of this butter and flour combination, store in a covered container in the refrigerator and stir a spoonful or so into pan drippings or soup to thicken. Kneaded butter makes the flour dissolve evenly into liquids and eliminates the problem of lumpy gravies and sauces.

> 1/4 cup soft butter
> 1/4 cup all-purpose flour

Mash together with a fork until very smooth. Scrape into a container, smooth the top, cover tightly and store in the refrigerator or use immediately. One tablespoon is sufficient to thicken 1 cup of gravy.

VEGETABLES

Carrots Glazed in Cider

      3 cups sliced, scraped carrots
      1/3 cup finely chopped onions
      2/3 cup fresh cider or apple juice
      2 tablespoons butter
      1/2 teaspoon salt
      2 tablespoons lemon juice
      2 teaspoons honey
      a few gratings of nutmeg

Combine the carrots, onions and cider in a saucepan. Cover and bring to the boil over high heat. Reduce the heat immediately to low and cook until the carrots are just tender, not mushy (about 10 minutes).

Uncover and add all the remaining ingredients except the nutmeg. Increase the heat to medium-high and cook, turning the carrots quite frequently, until the liquid has been absorbed and the carrots are glazed.

Turn into a warmed serving dish and grate a bit of nutmeg over the top. *Serves 5-6.*

Turnip-Apple Purée

      one 1 1/2 pound turnip (1 small or half a
            medium-large turnip)
      2 medium apples
      1/2 teaspoon salt
      1 cup chicken stock or water
      2 tablespoons butter
      2 tablespoons heavy cream
      1 tablespoon brown sugar
      1/4 teaspoon freshly ground pepper
      a few gratings of nutmeg (optional)

Peel, slice and dice the turnip into 3/4" cubes (approximately 4 cups).

Peel, core and slice the apples. There should be about 2 cups.

Place the turnip, apple, salt and stock in a medium saucepan. Cover and bring to the boil over high heat. Reduce the heat to low and simmer for 30 minutes or until the turnip is tender. Drain, reserving the liquid to use in soup or sauce.

Mash thoroughly and beat with an electric beater or press through a ricer or food mill to make the turnip as smooth and lump-free as possible.

Beat in the remaining ingredients and taste. Some turnips have a bitter taste and may need additional butter and sugar.

Serve hot immediately. This vegetable purée may be made in advance and reheated in a saucepan over gentle heat or in a greased heatproof dish, sprinkled with 1/2 cup buttered herbed crumbs (see page 82) and baked at 350 degrees for 30 minutes or until heated through.

Excellent with poultry (roasted chicken, duck, goose or turkey) as well as with all pork — chops, sausages or roasts. *Makes enough for 6.*

Sweet Potato - Apple Cider Casserole

    6 cups cooked, well mashed sweet potatoes
            (5-6 medium large potatoes)
    1/3 cup melted or very soft butter
    1/2 teaspoon salt
    1/4 teaspoon freshly ground pepper
    1/4 teaspoon freshly grated nutmeg
    1/4 teaspoon cinnamon
    3/4 cup fresh cider
    2 eggs, separated, plus 1 egg white
    2 tablespoons butter
    1/2 cup medium-fine breadcrumbs
    2 tablespoons finely chopped parsley

Combine the mashed sweet potatoes, melted butter, salt, spices, cider and egg yolks in a large mixing bowl. Mash thoroughly to remove any lumps and to blend the ingredients.

Beat the egg whites until they are stiff but not dry. Fold into the sweet potato mixture. Taste and add more salt, pepper or spices if desired. Turn into an ungreased 8-cup soufflé dish.

Melt the remaining butter and add the breadcrumbs and parsley. Stir to distribute the butter evenly. Sprinkle these buttered, herbed crumbs over the top of the potatoes.

Bake at 375 degrees for 40-45 minutes or until puffed up and crusty on top.

An excellent recipe for holiday buffets because all steps, up to the point of folding in the egg whites, can be done in advance. The crumbs also can be prepared ahead of time and sprinkled on just before baking. *Serves 10-12.*

Butter Sautéed Apple Rings

These are extremely easy to prepare and make an effective garnish for duck, goose, ham, most pork roasts and chops. A tart apple that keeps its shape during cooking is the best, and I suggest a Wolf River, Greening, Cortland or Northern Spy. Golden Delicious are good, but since they are sweeter, less sugar is required. Peach halves are surprisingly good, too; because of the short cooking period, they keep their fresh taste. This is a good accompaniment for chicken as well as the other meats suggested for the apples.

    2 large apples
    3 tablespoons butter
    1 1/2 tablespoons lemon juice
    2 tablespoons brown sugar
    cinnamon, nutmeg, mace or ginger
            (optional)

Wash the apples and cut a thin slice off the top and bottom. Divide each apple in 4 horizontally. Remove the core from each slice and pat the slices dry on paper towelling.

Melt the butter in a frying pan large enough to hold all the apple slices in 1 layer. When the butter bubbles up, add the apple slices. Adjust the heat so that the apples brown but the butter does not burn. Cook until golden-brown on 1 side, then turn over. Sprinkle the lemon juice and some of the brown sugar on each apple ring. Reduce the heat to low and cook 3-4 minutes more, or until the apples are just tender and the sugar melted. Dust lightly with a spice if desired.

Remove the apples with a turner, arrange as a garnish and pour the pan juices evenly over the apple rings.

Fried Peach Halves

Proceed as with Butter Sautéed Apple Rings but use 4 medium peaches, peeled, halved and stoned. (Canned peaches, well drained, are fine, too.) Sauté cut side down first, so that the sugar and lemon are in the hollow when finished sautéing. Serve as a garnish.

Savory Applesauce for Goose, Duck, Ham or Pork

4 cups peeled, cored, chopped apples
1/4 cup water
1/8 teaspoon cloves or allspice
1 tablespoon lemon juice or cider vinegar
1/4 cup firmly packed brown sugar
2 teaspoons butter

Combine the apples, water and cloves in a saucepan. Cover and cook over low heat until the apples are tender, then mash thoroughly. Uncover, increase the heat slightly and cook for 4-5 minutes to thicken. Stir constantly.

Mix in the lemon juice, sugar and butter. Serve hot.

Salads

We don't have to look at old cookbooks to know that Canadians have not traditionally been salad eaters. Most salads require an abundance of fresh vegetables, and it goes without saying that a year-round supply of fresh vegetables is a post-second world war phenomenon. Nevertheless, there are certain ingredients that went into familiar seasonal salads — watercress, leaf lettuce, radishes, dandelions and green onions in the spring; tomatoes, beans and cucumbers in the summer; and beets, cabbage, celery and apples in the fall and into the early winter months. Apples have played a surprisingly large part in our salad tradition, and while nowadays we are not forced to use them for salad, they still taste good with their traditional accompaniments — red or green cabbage, celery, beets and walnuts.

Waldorf Salad

1 1/2 cups chopped, cored, unpeeled, red-skinned apples
1 cup chopped celery, from the heart

1/2 cup fresh coarsely chopped walnuts
1 tablespoon lemon juice
1/4 teaspoon salt
1 cup mayonnaise
lettuce

Combine the apples, celery and walnuts. Sprinkle with the lemon juice and salt and gently mix in the mayonnaise. Spoon into lettuce cups and serve immediately. *Makes 4-6 servings.*

Cabbage and Apple Salad with Mustard Seed Dressing

4 cups finely shredded red or green cabbage
2 cups chopped, unpeeled, cored red-skinned apples
1/2 cup chopped celery
1/2 medium Spanish onion, sliced thinly
1/3 cup oil
2 tablespoons cider vinegar
2 teaspoons white sugar
1 teaspoon salt
1/4 teaspoon freshly ground pepper
1 teaspoon mustard seed
1 clove garlic, crushed

Combine the first 4 ingredients in a salad bowl. Mix the remaining ingredients for the dressing and pour over the cabbage and apples. Toss and chill 1 hour before serving. *Enough for 6-8 servings.*

Apple and Beet Salad

2 cups very finely shredded red cabbage
2$\frac{1}{2}$ cups unpeeled, cored, chopped, red-
    skinned apples
2 tablespoons lemon juice
2 cups cooked, peeled beets, chopped
    medium-fine
1$\frac{1}{2}$ cups finely chopped tender celery
3 tablespoons finely chopped green onions
$\frac{3}{4}$ cup mayonnaise
$\frac{1}{4}$ cup boiled dressing
$\frac{1}{4}$ cup commercial sour cream
1 teaspoon grated horseradish (optional)
$\frac{3}{4}$ teaspoon salt
$\frac{1}{4}$ teaspoon freshly ground pepper
1-2 teaspoons chopped fresh dill or $\frac{1}{4}$-$\frac{1}{2}$
    teaspoon dill seed

Arrange the cabbage in the bottom and halfway up the sides of a medium-large salad bowl. Toss the apples with the lemon juice and arrange in a circle around the edge of the bowl. Arrange the beets in a smaller circle. Combine the celery and onion and arrange in a still smaller circle, but leaving a 3"-4" well in the very centre of the bowl.

Mix together the mayonnaise, boiled dressing, sour cream, horseradish, salt and pepper. Fill the central well with this mixture. Sprinkle the dill over the dressing.

Bring to the table, toss thoroughly and serve. *Makes enough for 6-8.*

Creamy Apple Cabbage Salad with Walnuts and Raisins

5 cups shredded or chopped cabbage
1$\frac{1}{2}$ cups chopped, unpeeled, cored red-
    skinned apples (or pears, cored and
    peeled)
$\frac{1}{4}$ cup chopped onions
$\frac{1}{4}$ cup chopped celery
$\frac{1}{3}$ cup raisins
$\frac{1}{3}$ cup coarsely chopped fresh walnuts
2 tablespoons lemon juice
1-1$\frac{1}{4}$ cups mayonnaise
salt and freshly ground pepper

Combine all the ingredients except the mayonnaise, salt and pepper in a large salad bowl. Mix in enough of the mayonnaise to make a creamy salad. Add salt and pepper to taste. Chill 1 hour before serving. *Serves 8-10.*

DRINKS AND CANDY

Cider Cup

"This is a novel and delicious 'cup' for a garden party or an 'at home'," according to the *Modern Household Cookery Book*, published in Vancouver at the turn of the century. The ingredients in this recipe suggest that some garden parties must have been merry affairs.

> 3/4 tray of ice cubes
> 4-5 very thin slices of lemon
> 4-5 very thin slices of unpeeled cucumber
> 1/4 cup brandy
> 1/4 cup orange liqueur
> 2 1/2 cups sparkling, dry cider
> 3 cups ginger beer (the hot West Indian kind is excellent)

Place the ice in the bottom of a chilled punch bowl. Add the lemon, cucumber, brandy and orange liqueur. Mix. Add the cider and ginger beer. Stir lightly, and serve when chilled but still very bubbly. Serve a slice of lemon or cucumber in each cup. *Serves 6-8.*

Multiply the quantities for large gatherings. The amount of cider and ginger beer can be increased if a less alcoholic "cup" is desired.

Sparkling Cider and Cranberry Cooler

> 1/2 teaspoon grated orange rind
> 2 1/2 cups cranberries
> 3 cups water
> 2/3 cup white sugar
> 3 tablespoons lemon juice
> 1 cup orange juice
> 6 thin orange slices
> 1/3-2/3 cup vodka
> 2 cups medium-sweet sparkling cider
> 1/4-1/2 teaspoon bitters
> ice

To make the cranberry juice, combine the first 3 ingredients in a saucepan. Cover and bring to the boil over high heat. Reduce heat and simmer 10 minutes or until all the cranberries have popped. Strain through a fine sieve or jelly bag.

Combine the cranberry juice and sugar in a clean saucepan. Heat just enough to dissolve the sugar. Cool.

To complete the cooler, combine with the juices, orange slices and vodka. Store in the refrigerator until serving time.

Pour into a punch bowl, add the cider and the 1/4 teaspoon bitters. Shake in more bitters if desired. Add ice and serve. *Enough for 6 as a punch.*

Hot Mulled Cider

2 quarts fresh apple cider (10 cups)
$1/2$ lemon, cut in thin slices
one 3" cinnamon stick
$1/4$ cup firmly packed brown sugar
additional lemon slices or cinnamon sticks
(optional)

Combine the cider, lemon and cinnamon in a saucepan. Bruise the lemon slices with the back of a wooden spoon. Bring to the boil, reduce heat and simmer for 10 minutes. Remove the lemon and cinnamon and add the sugar. Taste and add more sugar if desired.

Serve with a fresh slice of lemon or a stick of cinnamon in tea glasses or mugs. This mulled cider is also good cold with ice cubes. *Makes 10-12 servings.*

Rolling Peaches in Sparkling Wine

one 26 ounce bottle of sparkling, medium,
white wine
4-6 small, ripe, juicy freestone peaches
2-3 tablespoons brandy

Chill the wine and 4-6 deep wine glasses which are wide enough to accommodate the peaches.

Peel the peaches and prick all over, right to the stone with a fork. Place in a bowl, sprinkle on the brandy, cover and chill 1 hour. Turn 2-3 times.

To serve, place one peach in each glass, dividing the juice evenly among the glasses. Fill the glasses with wine. The bubbling wine makes the peaches roll in the glass, hence the name.

Serve immediately. This is almost a dessert, so supply spoons to eat the peaches when the wine is gone.

Hot Rum and Cider

4 cups fresh apple cider
$1/2$ orange, cut in thin slices
8 whole cloves
two 3" cinnamon sticks
3-4 tablespoons brown sugar (optional)
$1/2$ cup rum
additional cinnamon sticks or orange slices

Combine the first 4 ingredients in a saucepan. Bruise the orange slices with the back of a wooden spoon. Bring to the boil, reduce the heat to low and simmer for 10 minutes. Remove orange and spices. Taste and add the brown sugar if desired. Mix in the rum.

Serve in mugs or tea glasses with a fresh orange slice or cinnamon stick in each mug. *Enough for 6.*

Thick Peach Milk Shake

$1/4$ cup orange juice
2 fresh peaches, peeled and chopped
$1/4$ cup white sugar
$11/2$ cups vanilla ice cream
$2/3$ cup milk
freshly grated nutmeg or orange rind

Combine all the ingredients except the nutmeg in a blender. Cover and blend 20 seconds or until creamy and smooth. Pour into chilled glasses and grate nutmeg over the top.

Drained, canned peaches or pears can be substituted for the fresh peaches, but reduce the sugar to 2 tablespoons. *Serves 3.*

Apple Allies

It seemed preposterous that, despite all our apples, the only recipes for candy are for taffy apples. So I was delighted to come across this 60-year-old recipe in Victoria, British Columbia. The best apples for Allies are the ones that hold their shape during cooking; I recommend Yellow Delicious and Cortlands. The Yellow Delicious turn bright yellow when cooked and look quite unusual.

> 1 cup white sugar
> $1/2$ cup water
> 2-3 drops cinnamon oil or one 3" cinnamon
>   stick (optional)
> 4-5 medium apples
> approximately $1/2$ cup white sugar

Combine the 1 cup sugar, water and oil in a wide, shallow saucepan. Stir and bring to the boil over medium heat. Reduce the heat so that the syrup bubbles gently.

Peel, quarter and core one of the apples. Divide each quarter into 3 sections and drop into the syrup. Cook only one layer of apple slices at a time. When the slices are transparent and easily pierced with a skewer, remove with a slotted spoon. Let excess syrup drip back into the saucepan. Spread the apples out on aluminum foil or waxed paper. Repeat with the remaining apples, adding a little more boiling water if necessary to keep the syrup at the same consistency. Control the heat carefully so that the syrup does not begin to caramelize. By the time all the apples have been boiled the syrup will have all been used up.

Let the apples stand for 24 hours on the foil in a cool, dry, airy part of the kitchen. Sprinkle 2-3 tablespoons of sugar over the allies, turning each one over to coat both sides. Let stand for 24 hours more and then roll again in sugar. Repeat the 24 hour rest and the sugar rolling procedure once more. Let the apples remain on the foil until they are completely dry. Replace the foil if moisture accumulates on it.

When all the slices are dry and crystalline in appearance, pack them into airtight containers. *Yields 60 slices of candy.*

Taffy Apples

Taffy apples date back to the time when people made molasses-pull taffy, chocolate fudge and maple cream not just for the eating, but for the pleasure of being together. I recommend making taffy apples with a bunch of enthusiastic kids who don't have to worry about their fillings falling out.

> $11/2$ cups white sugar
> $1/2$ cup corn syrup
> $2/3$ cup water
> $1/2$ teaspoon cider vinegar
> 12 medium-small apples
> 12 wooden skewers
> 1 teaspoon vanilla or 2-3 drops cinnamon oil

Combine the first 4 ingredients in a deep heavy-bottomed saucepan. Place over medium heat and stir just to dissolve the sugar. Don't stir at all during the rest of the cooking period. Bring slowly to the boil and reduce the heat to low. Boil to 290 degrees on a candy thermometer, just as it reaches the hard crack stage. To test candy without a candy thermometer, drip a bit of the candy into a glass of cold water. When the drops harden, become brittle and can be broken, remove the taffy from the heat. Watch the bubbling taffy carefully as it boils. Do not increase the heat to hurry up the boiling or the taffy will burn and become inedible.

While the taffy is cooking, wash and wipe the apples. Remove the stems and push a wooden skewer firmly into the cores. Grease a 2' length of aluminum foil and place it on a baking sheet.

When the taffy has reached the correct temperature, remove immediately from the heat and stir in the flavouring. Dip the apples one at a time very quickly into the taffy and set, wooden skewer up, on the greased foil. Leave 2"-3" between the apples. Always dip as quickly as possible as the high heat of the taffy will cook the apples and destroy the desired effect of a brittle, slightly caramel taffy over crisp juicy apple.

Some recipes recommend setting the saucepan with the cooked taffy into a larger shallow pan of very hot water. This helps to keep the taffy from hardening before all the apples are dipped — a good idea if children are helping.

VARIETIES

Apples

Variety	Season	Characteristics	Uses
Yellow Transparent	First 3 weeks of August	Light green to pale yellow with a tart flavour. The flesh tends to be mealy if too ripe. Smaller than later apples.	Very good cooking apple, especially for a smooth sauce. Just fair for eating.
Lodi	Mid-August	Tart, juicy, crisp early apple, a little larger than the Transparent (it is a descendent of the Transparent), but has a similar green-yellow colour.	Cooks up smoothly and very white with a good flavour. Good for sherbets and applesauce. Fair eating.
Red Astrachan	Last 3 weeks of August	Often very small. Has a powerful fragrance and tasty flesh. The skin is a delicate red with some yellow.	Use for cooking because of the fine flavour. Excellent for sauces and pies.
Melba	Late August, early September	Really an early McIntosh, it is the firmest of the early apples. Bright streaky red with a juicy, very white crunchy flesh. Medium to above average size.	Good for cooking and superior for eating.
Duchess	Late August	An old-fashioned apple with an excellent flavour. Its skin is light green with red stripes and splashes	Good cooking apple worth looking for at farmers' markets. Makes sensational pies.
Early McIntosh	Late August until mid- to late September	A cross between the Yellow Transparent and the McIntosh, this is a predominately red apple with a crisp flesh. Not considered as good as the McIntosh.	Good dessert apple, fair for cooking.
Wealthy	Mid-September until November	Bright red skin with greenish-yellow stripes. Tart and aromatic flesh, slightly tinged with pink.	Excellent cooking apple, average for dessert.

Gravenstein	Mid-September to November	Red blush with some yellow stripes. Good-sized. The skin is slightly rough, and the flesh is yellowish, firm and crisp. These attractive apples do not ripen all at the same time. Very popular in Nova Scotia.	Superior cooking apple.
Crabapples	Late September until late November	Small, hard apple with yellowish flesh and yellow to bright red skin.	Recommended for pickling and jelly.
McIntosh	Mid-September until early spring	*The* Canadian apple. The skin is red, the shape slightly irregular, and the aroma distinctive, especially early in the fall. White, firm, crisp and extremely juicy flesh. Has a tendency to develop a tough skin and flat taste after long storage.	An excellent dessert apple. Suitable for cooking in sauce type recipes when you do not want the apple to keep its shape. The flesh browns quickly when exposed to the air.
Lobo	September to November	Flat red and green apple with a crisp white flesh. A McIntosh seedling popular in Quebec and New Brunswick.	Good for cooking and dessert.
Cortland	Early October until early winter	Red skin, white flesh and a slightly flat shape. A descendent of the McIntosh, but the fruit is larger. Popular in eastern Canada.	Good for cooking, especially for salads as it doesn't brown quickly. Fine for desserts as well.
Rhode Island Greening	Early October until late December	Bright green skin with white, rather tart flesh. Large and firm. Popular in the last century, it has regained market appeal since the importation of the Granny Smith apple. Rather flat flavour.	Because this apple keeps its shape well, it is excellent for baked apples, and its tartness makes for good jelly. Not recommended for eating.
Tolman Sweet	Early October until mid-winter	Yellow, smallish apples that have a distinctively sweet smell and taste. The skin is smooth and waxy.	Excellent dessert apple and one of the best for pickling. Keeps its shape during cooking.

Idared	Mid-October until mid-spring	Very smooth-skinned red apple which is a descendent of the Jonathon and Wagener apples. Because of its ability to remain in good condition in storage, it is currently being recommended to growers.	Good dessert and cooking apple.
Spartan	Mid-October until late winter	Very crisp, juicy flesh. Bright red skin, sweet flavour and round shape. Becoming more popular with growers and consumers, especially in British Columbia and Ontario.	Cooks smoothly and retains its flavour. Superior dessert apple.
King	Mid-October until mid-winter	Distinctive because of its large size. Orange-red to deep-red in colour with a few stripes. Like the Northern Spy, the trees take a long time to bear fruit. Common in Nova Scotia.	Good cooking and salad apple, but only fair for eating raw.
Wagener	Mid-October until February	Light red skin. This apple is high in Vitamin C. Popular in Nova Scotia.	Fair dessert apple. It retains its shape in cooking. Can be a high quality apple if well grown, but losing popularity in recent years.
Red Delicious	Mid-October until spring	Red-skinned with an elongated shape and the distinctive five points on the bottom. The flesh is very juicy and sweet and quite tasty, especially early in the season.	Primarily a dessert apple.
Northern Spy	Mid-October until spring	Striped red skin, creamy yellow, crisp, juicy flesh. Harvested just before the heavy frosts, it keeps well in storage. It has a distinctive aroma.	The best winter cooking apple because it holds its shape. It also makes a smooth sauce or a tasty dessert apple.
Golden Delicious	Mid-October until early spring	Sweet, juicy and very tasty, this apple has an overpowering fragrance, especially early in the season. It is yellow and elongated with the distinctive five points on the blossom end.	Excellent dessert apple, especially when it has not been stored too long. Although not considered good for cooking, it is very successful in recipes where it is important for the apple to keep its shape.

Snow (Fameuse)	Mid-October in Ontario until mid-winter in Quebec	Pure, snowy-white flesh with a scarlet red skin. Often quite small. Still popular in Quebec.	Excellent for dessert and most cooking purposes. Good for jelly and sauce recipes where the skin is cooked in with the flesh.
(Golden) Russet	Mid-October until late winter	Rough golden-green-brown skin with a creamy, very juicy flesh. These apples tend to be small and to wrinkle in storage. Nevertheless the taste and fragrance are so good that it deserves to be noticed.	Good for dessert, cider, pickling and cooking. Keeps its shape in cooking. An ideal apple to serve with nuts and cheese.
Rome Beauty, Red Rome	Mid-October until late winter	Bright red, round apple with hard white flesh. Becoming popular, although the taste is disappointing after storage.	Generally good, all-purpose apple.
Newtown	Picked in October, available until April	Bright lime-green skin, round shape and firm, very white flesh. It has a tangy taste and is quite juicy. Popular in British Columbia, partly because it stores well.	Good cooking apple if not too ripe. Fair for eating.
Winesap	Picked in October, available until May	Very firm flesh with a tart flavour and bright red skin. Stores well.	Excellent for cooking in recipes where it is important for the apple to keep its shape as in pies.

I have tried to choose the most common varieties from across the country, but of course many new varieties are being developed all the time and many old varieties improved.

Peaches

Variety	Season	Characteristics·	Uses
Dixired	Late July	Juicy, yellow clingstone peach.	Best eaten fresh.
Erlyvee	Late July	Juicy, sweet flavour. Clingstone with a creamy yellow skin and red blush. Small in size. Grown in Essex and Kent counties in Ontario.	Good eaten fresh, for brandied peaches or for canning.
Sunhaven	Early August	A semi-clingstone peach with a juicy, sweet flavour and creamy yellow skin and red blush. Smallish in size.	Good eaten fresh, for brandied peaches or for canning.
Redhaven	Mid-August	A very juicy freestone with yellow skin and lovely red blush. Its sweet flavour makes it one of the best tasting peaches.	Excellent for eating fresh, freezing or preserving.
Golden Jubilee	Mid-August to early September	A yellow-skinned freestone, generally processed now because consumers prefer a red peach. Very good flavour and very juicy.	Good fresh and for all cooking purposes and freezing.
Loring	Mid-August to early September	A freestone peach with a yellow skin and red blush. Good flavour.	Recommended for freezing, preserving and eating fresh.
Valiant, Veteren, Vedette, Velvet	Mid- to late August	The freestone "Vee" peaches developed at Vineland, Ontario.	Good general purpose peach. Best for canning.
Fairhaven	Mid- to late August	A freestone with a yellow skin and red blush.	General purpose.
Elberta	Early to mid-September	A yellow, fairly juicy peach.	Good for eating and preserving.
Madison	Mid-September	A yellow-skinned, quite juicy peach with coarser flesh than most.	Good for eating and preserving.
Redskin	Mid-September	A big, yellow-skinned peach. Quite juicy flesh, but not as fine as early peaches.	Good for eating and preserving.

Pears

Variety	Season	Characteristics	Uses
Lawson Gifford	Early August	Juicy.	A good dessert pear.
Clapp's Favourite	Mid-August to September	A yellow, very juicy, fragrant pear, very popular in Nova Scotia.	A good dessert pear.
Bartlett	Late August to mid-September; in storage until late winter	A firm, juicy, full-flavoured pear with slightly spotty skin, turning from green to yellow when ripe. Some varieties have a red skin. Most of the Ontario crop is marketed fresh, the Nova Scotia crop processed and much of the B.C. crop kept in storage to supply winter and early spring markets.	Good for desserts, canning, pickling and cooking.
Anjou	Late September; in storage until the end of the winter	A bulbous-shaped pear, light green in colour with a yellow tinge.	Primarily a dessert pear.
Flemish Beauty	Mid-September; in storage until early winter	A juicy, yellow-skinned pear with a red blush. It matures well in storage (some people feel it is better after storage than fresh-picked).	Good for desserts and cooking.
Bosc	End of September; in storage until late winter	A characteristically long, tapered neck with russet brown skin. Very juicy and tasty.	Good for desserts, cooking and pickling.
Keiffer (Keifer)	September to October	Yellow-skinned with slightly gritty flesh. Buy on local markets, as the bulk of the crop is sold directly to processors.	The best cooking pear as it keeps its shape.
Seckel or sugar pear	September to October	A small, brownish-rusty coloured pear with a humpy shape.	Primarily suited to canning and pickling.

Practical Metric Conversion Table
VOLUME MEASURES

Imperial	Metric
1 pint	slightly more than 500 ml.
1 quart	1.12 l
1 cup	250 ml
1/2 cup	125 ml
1/3 cup	75 ml
1 tablespoon	15 ml
1 teaspoon	5 ml
1/2 teaspoon	2 ml (rounded)
1/4 teaspoon	1 ml (rounded)

LINEAR MEASURES

1 inch	2.5 cm

MASS

1 ounce	28 gr
1 pound	0.45 kg

TEMPERATURE

Fahrenheit	Celsius
500	260
450	230
400	200
375	190
350	180
300	150
250	120
200	95
150	65

INDEX

Apples

Cakes
Apple and Nut Sour Cream Coffee
  Cake 13
Apple Butter Sponge Roll 20
Apple Ginger Upside-Down
  Cake 14
Apple Meringue Cake 12
Applesauce Cake 12
Apple Wedge Maple Syrup
  Upside-Down Cake 14
Dried Apple Cake 17
Dutch Apple, Peach or Pear
  Cake 16
Hustling Harvesters' Cake 16
Layered Cinnamon Apple Coffee
  Cake 12
Raisin Layer Apple Jack 11
Spicy Apple Nut Coffee Cake 14

Drinks and Candy
Apple Allies 86
Cider Cup 85
Hot Mulled Cider 86
Hot Rum and Cider 86
Sparkling Cider and Cranberry
  Cooler 85
Taffy Apples 87

Garnishes
Butter Sautéed Apple Rings 82
Savory Applesauce for Goose, Duck,
  Ham or Pork 83

Meat and Fish Main Courses
Apple and Tarragon Stuffed
  Whitefish 80
Cider and Apple Chicken 76
Cider Sauced Butterfly Pork
  Chops 78
Cinnamon Pork Chops 78
Pork and Apple Pie 78
Roast Butt of Pork with Prune and
  Apple Stuffing 76
Roast Turkey with Applesauce
  Sausage Dressing 74
Sauerkraut Dressed Duck 75

Muffins, Quickbreads and Pancakes
Apple Butter Pound Cake 23
Apple Nut Muffins 21
Apple Nut or Apple Raisin Bread 22
Apple or Peach Pancakes 25
Applesauce Streusel Muffins 21
Cider Pound Cake 22
Cranberry Apple Bread 22
Molasses Hot Applesauce Bread 22

Pickles, Relishes and Preserves
Amber Fruit Sauce 61
Apple Fresh Herb Jellies 64
Apple Jelly 64
Apple Juice for Jelly Making 64
Cranberry and Apple Jelly 66
Drying Apples 72
Elderberry and Apple Jelly 65
Elderberry Juice for Jelly Making 65
Fresh Apple-Cranberry Relish 63
Gingery Apple and Ripe Tomato
  Chutney 61
Mild Spiced Crabapples 63
Preserved Applesauce 70
Red Apple and Green Tomato
  Barbecue Sauce 62
Rich Mincemeat 72
Spiced Crabapple Jelly 65
West Coast Apple Ginger Sauce 67

Pies
Apple and Elderberry Pie 38
Apple Butter Pie 36
Apple Cranberry Nut Pie 37
Apple Dumplings or Paddy
  Bundles 34
Apple Turnover Deluxe 35
August Apple and Peach Pie 36
Caramel Apple Pie 39
Classic Apple Pie 28
Custard Top Dried Apple Pie 38
Deep Dish Apple Pie 29
Fruit Mincemeat Pie 31
Helen Harris' Upside-Down Apple
  Pie 34
John Clements' Jelly Apple Pie 32
Rich Mincemeat Pie 30
Sour Cream Apple Pie 32

Cookies
Apple and Nut Squares 26
Apple Rolled Oats Squares 25
Applesauce Spice Hermits 26

Puddings, Ice Creams and Sherbets
Apple Betty 54
Apple Charlotte 54
Apple Custard Meringue 57
Apple Float 42
Apple Ginger Ice Cream 50
Apple Honey Sherbet 51
Apple Pan Dowdy 58
Apple Souffle 42
Apple Trifle 44
Bird's Nest Pudding 56
Cranberry Applesauce 41
Dried Apple and Prune
  Compote 45
Elderberry or Grape Apple or Pear
  Sauce 41
Fresh Apple Cider and Cranberry
  Jelly 48
Fresh Apple Slices in Green Ginger
  Syrup 59
Honey Deluxe Apple Crisp 53
Honey Pear and Applesauce 41
Maple Baked Apples 45
Meringue Apple Pudding 57
Mincemeat Baked Apples 46
Nut-Meringue Maple Baked
  Apples 46
Simple Baked Apples 45
Steamed Apple Pudding 58
Swedish Apple Pudding 55
Sweetened Applesauce 41
Thick Unsweetened Applesauce 11

Salads
Waldorf Salad 83
Cabbage and Apple Salad with
  Mustard Seed Dressing 83
Apple and Beet Salad 84

Creamy Apple Cabbage Salad with
  Walnuts and Raisins   84

Vegetables
Carrots Glazed in Cider   81
Sweet Potato-Apple Cider
  Casserole   82
Turnip-Apple Purée   81

Peaches

Cakes
Classic Peach Shortcake   18
Dutch Apple, Peach or Pear
  Cake   16
Peach Cream Delight   18
Upside-Down Peach Cake   15

Drinks
Rolling Peaches in Sparkling
  Wine   86
Thick Peach Milk Shake   86

Garnishes
Fried Peach Halves   82

Pancakes and Fritters
Apple or Peach Pancakes   25
Peach Doughnuts   24
Peach Fritters   24

Pickles, Relishes and Preserves
Amber Fruit Sauce   61
Brandied Peach Marmalade   68
Brandied Peaches   68
Classic Peach Marmalade   68
Frozen Peaches   71
Home Canned Peaches   70
Peach and Grape Jam   66
Peach and Raisin Conserve   68
Peach and Red Pepper Relish   60
Spiced Peaches   62

Pies
August Apple and Peach Pie   36
Classic Peach Pie   28
Deep Dish Fresh Peach Pie   30
Fresh Peach Tarts   40
Fruit Mincemeat Pie   31
Olive Davis' Schnitz Peach Pie   32
Peach Apricot Meringue Pie   39
Peach Custard Pie   32

Puddings, Ice Creams and Sherbets

Baked Peaches with Slivered
  Almonds   46

Fresh Peach Ice Water   52
Fresh Peach Mould   46
Peaches and Ice Cream in Almond
  Meringues   52
Peach Foam   43
Peach Ice Cream   50
Peach Trifle   43
Peach Velvet   49

Pears

Cakes
Dutch Apple, Peach, or Pear Cake   16

Pickles, Relishes and Preserves
Amber Fruit Sauce   61
Honey Pear Butter with Rum   66
Pear and Raisin Conserve   68
Pear Chutney   62
Pear Mincemeat   73
Preserved Pears   70

Pies
Figgy Pear Tarts   40
Golden Honey Pear Pie   29
Pear and Elderberry Pie   38
Pear and Ginger Pie   31
Pear and Mincemeat Pie   31

Puddings and Sherbets
Elderberry or Grape Apple or Pear
  Sauce   41
Honey Pear and Applesauce   41
Meringue of Pears   56
Moulded Pears in Port   48
Mrs. Beeton's Stewed Pears in
  Port   44
Oven Baked Pears   46
Pear Ice Water   52

Miscellaneous

Almond Meringues   53
Caramel Sauce   59
Classic Butter Cake   19
Cream Cheese Icing   17
Custard Sauce   42
Hot Water Pastry   27
Kneaded Butter   80
Maple Butter Sauce   25
Sponge Cake   18
Standard Pastry   27
Walnut Rum Butter Icing   12